Editor:
Janet Cain, M.Ed.

Editorial Project Manager:
Elizabeth Morris, Ph.D.

Editor in Chief:
Sharon Coan, M.S. Ed.

Cover Artist:
Sue Fullam

Art Coordinator:
Cheri Macoubrie Wilson

Creative Director:
Elayne Roberts

Imaging:
James Edward Grace

Product Manager:
Phil Garcia

Publishers:
Rachelle Cracchiolo, M.S. Ed.
Mary Dupuy Smith, M.S. Ed.

PRIMARY

Author:

Alyssa Weller

Teacher
Created
Materials

Teacher Created Materials, Inc.
6421 Industry Way
Westminster, CA 92683
www.teachercreated.com

©1999 Teacher Created Materials, Inc.
Reprinted, 2000
Made in U.S.A.
ISBN-1-57690-461-X

Table of Contents

Introduction

Computer Activities A-Z is a book filled with exciting technology projects that are fun and motivational for primary students. This book includes activities that can easily be integrated into the existing curriculum. Students utilize language arts, math, science, and social studies skills when doing these projects. In addition, students have opportunities to improve their ability to use a mouse, keyboard, printer, as well as graphics and word-processing software.

All of the activities are created to be age-appropriate and motivational for primary students. They are user-friendly for teachers who are just beginning to implement technology into their lessons as well as for those who are very experienced.

Many of the activities in this book are projects that were created by my mother, Bonnie Tadelman. They have been adapted for use with computers. My mother was a nurturing, creative kindergarten teacher for 19 years before passing away in 1994. Her dedication and enthusiasm for teaching has been a true inspiration to me in my teaching career. I hope that you enjoy the projects in *Computer Activities A-Z* and that these projects will inspire you to use technology with your students.

How to Use This Book

A comprehensive list of projects and activities is available in the table of contents (page 2). This list can be used to match your projects by name to the themes or units that you teach. If you teach a letter per week, you can refer to the projects alphabetically (pages 12 and 13).

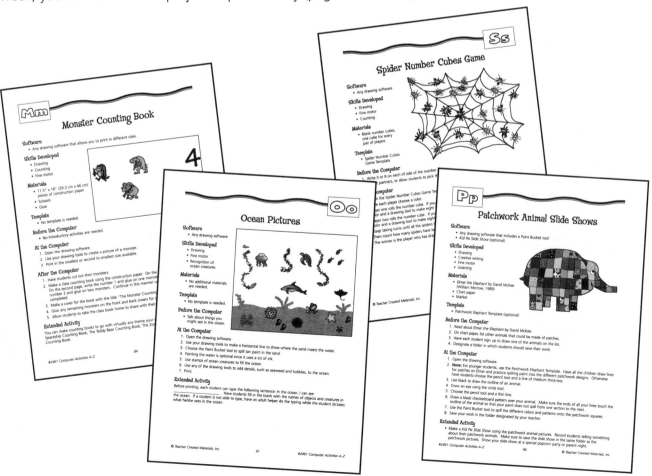

Software Recommendations

The projects and templates recommended in this book are very versatile because they can be used with a variety of children's software. Each project specifies the type of software needed. Some software recommendations are listed below.

Drawing Software

- *Kid Pix, Kid Pix Studio,* or *Kid Pix Deluxe*
Available from Broderbund Software—
(800) 521-6263

- *Kid Works 2 or Kid Works Deluxe*
Available from Davidson and Associates, Inc.—
(800) 545-7677

- *Claris Works for Kids*
Available from Claris Corp.—
(408) 727-8227

- *Stanley's Sticker Book*
Available from Edmark—
(800) 362-2890

- *Creative Writer*
Available from Microsoft Corp.—
(800) 227-4679

- *The Children's Writing Center*
Available from The Learning Corp.—
(800) 852-2255

- *Student Writing Center*
Available from The Learning Corp.—
(800) 852-2255

- *The Writing Center*
Available from The Learning Corp.—
(800) 852-2255

Graphing Software

- *The Graph Club*
Available from Tom Snyder Productions—
(800) 342-0236

Word-Processing Software

- *Amazing Writing Machine*
Available from Broderbund Software, Inc.—
(800) 474-8840

- *Bank Street Writer*
Available from Scholastic Software—
(800) 541-5513

- *Claris Works for Kids*
Available from Claris Corp.—
(408) 727-8227

Font Software

- *Fontastics and Fontastics II*
Available from DJ Inkers—
(800) 325-4890

Other Useful Software

- *The Print Shop Deluxe*
Available from Broderbund Software, Inc.—
(800) 474-8840

- *Super Print II*
Available from Scholastic Software—
(800) 541-5513

Class Books

Class books are definitely an asset to your technology curriculum. Your students will gain a sense of accomplishment when they see all of their hard work published in book form. They will also be excited to bring these books home to share with their families. Class books provide students with extra reading and listening practice outside of school. In addition parents will be pleased to see that technology has been put to good use in your classroom.

Types of Class Books

Class books can be made in any size or form. Large books are fun for displaying special oversized projects. Regular-sized books are practical for easy transport in book bags. Miniature books are fun and easy for little hands to hold. For a special treat, make a shape book by mounting computer projects on construction paper and cutting out the pages in a shape, such as a dinosaur, that goes with a particular unit of study.

Ways to Bind Books

There are many ways of binding class books. Some suggestions are provided below. Using a variety of methods will keep your students interested in the book-making process. Remember that books can be bound on the left-hand side or at the top.

- **Spirals**—If you have a binding machine available at your school, a spiral binding will give your books a very professional finish.
- **Metal Rings**—You can bind your books with two or three metal rings. These rings are available at office or teacher supply stores. Use a hole puncher to punch holes in each page, making sure the holes line up. Reinforcers are recommended, especially on the front and back covers.
- **Yarn Bows**—Bows can add a festive flair to your books. Use a hole puncher to punch holes in each page, making sure the holes line up. Again, reinforcers are recommended, especially on the front and back covers. **Note:** Books that are bound with yarn bows are difficult to repair if any pages fall out.
- **Folders**—For quick, sturdy books, punch holes and place your pages in folders with brass brads. You may wish to write the title of the book on the front of the folder.

Class Books *(cont.)*

Organization

Use a checklist to keep track of when each student takes a book home and when he/she returns the book to school. When every student has had an opportunity to take a particular class book home, place that book in the classroom library for students to use during free time or silent reading.

Other Helpful Suggestions

1. Students can draw their portraits on a special class-made table of contents. To do this, divide a paper into rectangles. Write one student's name in each rectangle. Invite students to draw pictures of their faces next to their names. Then reproduce the title page so it can be placed at the beginning of each class book. You may wish to add page numbers next to each student's picture, indicating on which page his/her work can be found.

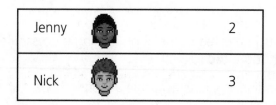

2. Remember to leave a margin along the left-hand side or at the top in order to bind your book. That way you will not cover up any of the text or pictures.

3. For easy transport, send home the class books in large resealable plastic bags. For larger books, plastic shopping bags with handles are helpful. As an alternative you may wish to buy clear plastic hanging book bags with handles. These are available from many book supply stores.

4. Number the pages of each book to give students extra practice with number recognition. Students love to see on which page their picture appears. They also have fun finding the pages with their friends' pictures.

5. If you have photographs of your students, you can add these to the pages they make. This is an excellent way to help students who cannot read find the pages that their friends have made.

6. Leave a blank page in the back of each book for parents to write their comments on. These comments are fun to read when the class books are brought back to school.

7. Place a copy of the letter to parents (page 7) in the bag when you send a book home with a student. This letter provides parents with suggestions for ways to share the book with their child.

8. Class books make a great display for open house, back-to-school night, or other parent nights. You can also display class books for parent-teacher conferences. Simply put a desk and chairs outside your classroom. Place an assortment of class-made books on the desk. Encourage parents to read the books while they are waiting for their assigned conference time.

9. Create and enjoy these very precious books all year long.

Parent Letter

Date

Dear Parents,

It is our pleasure to share this special class-made book with you. We are very excited for you to see it. Please treat it with care while you have it at home. Below are some suggestions for ways to enjoy this book with your child.

1. Read the book to your child, with your child, or have your child read the book to you.

2. Help your child find the page on which his/her work is shown. Together read the page number. Ask your child to tell about his/her page. Then have your child tell how he/she made this special page.

3. Ask your child to find some of the pages created by his/her friends. Help your child read these page numbers.

4. Have your child point out a page that he/she really likes. Ask your child to tell what he/she likes about that page.

5. Encourage your child to point out any words in the book that he/she knows how to read. Then ask your child to pick the three words that are the hardest for him/her to read. Read these aloud to your child.

6. Tell your child at least three things that you liked about the book. Please take a few seconds to write something on the parent comment page, which is located in the back of the book.

Thank you for taking the time to read our class-made book. Please don't forget to send the book back to our class with your child so another youngster will have the opportunity to take it home.

Sincerely,

_____

Teacher

_____

School

_____

Phone

Managing Technology

The activities presented in this book can be adapted to fit your needs. Whether your students use computers in a lab setting or in your classroom, listed below and on page 9 are some easy tips to help you implement technology into your daily lessons.

Tips for Using Computers in a Lab Setting

1. Before your students enter the lab, give instructions or do the Before the Computer activity with them. This way you will have your students' full attention while you are trying to give instructions. If there is a computer you can use for demonstration purposes, you may wish to show students how the project is done. Otherwise, you can show them a sample of the completed project.

2. You can minimize the noise level in the computer lab using a prearranged silent signal system so that students have a way of letting you know when they need help or they want you to review their work. This procedure can be as simple as a student placing a plastic cup upside-down on the top of the computer monitor when she/he needs you. When you are done working with that student, remind her/him to place the cup on the table next to the computer. Feel free to use any system that works well for you and your students.

3. Have the children work together in the computer lab whenever possible. Peer tutoring and collaborative work can be a very positive experience. Children enjoy working together and teaching each other new things. When children work with partners or in small groups, motivation is increased and their need for teacher assistance is minimized.

4. Utilizing parent and community volunteers is often beneficial when working with children in a computer lab setting. For more complicated projects, you may find it helpful to have additional adults or older students available to provide assistance to students.

8

Managing Technology *(cont.)*

Tips for Using Computers in a Classroom Setting

1. If you have one or more computers in your classroom, you can set up a computer center for students to use. Activities for this center can be explained to the whole group. Then the children can complete the lesson during work time or while other activities are going on in the classroom.

2. When only one computer is available in the classroom, post a list of students' names on a clipboard at the computer. Students should cross off their names when they are finished. After a child has just had a turn at the computer he/she should check to see whose name is next on the list. Then he/she should quietly tell the next student that the computer is available. This way students can use the computer center while other activities are taking place.

3. Arrange computers so that two chairs can fit in front of each computer monitor. Use masking tape to mark off an area around the computers. All students who are waiting for a turn or who are watching the computer can stand behind the line. This gives students on the computer enough room to manipulate the mouse and complete their projects.

4. Students should work together on classroom computers whenever possible. Peer tutoring and collaborative work can be a very positive experience. Students enjoy working together and teaching each other new things. When students work with partners or in small groups, motivation is increased and their need for teacher assistance is minimized.

5. Utilizing parent and community volunteers is often beneficial when working with children in a computer lab setting. For more complicated projects, you may find it helpful to have additional adults or older students available to provide assistance to students.

Other Helpful Tips

1. Before you begin any project, allow students to explore the software that they will be using.

2. Save student projects on the hard drives or diskettes and print them later, when students are not in the room. This maximizes the amount of time your students have using the computers.

3. Save ink by only printing special projects. Do not allow students to print pictures that they make during their free time.

4. Turn down the sound on the computers or have headphones available for students to use.

5. Remind left-handed students to move the mouse and mouse pad to the left-hand side of the keyboard before they begin.

Tips for Using Slide Shows

Slide shows are a wonderful way to use technology in your class. They can be used to introduce your students to multimedia projects. Your students will love being able to use as much color as they want in their slide show pictures. Slide shows are an excellent way to show off student work. In addition, they save on paper and ink because you do not have to print out anything for display.

Tips for Teachers

1. Prior to beginning the project, make a special folder on your hard drive or diskette for all your students' pictures. Then be sure to save all the pictures and the final slide show in that folder. **Note:** Once you make the slide show, it will not run unless you keep those pictures in the folder with it.

2. If you are making a class slide show where each student makes a picture for the show, remember to make a special title slide to use as your first slide.

3. Slide shows can be recorded to videotape so that your students can take home the tape to share with their families. You can also print out slide show pictures to make a class book that can be sent home. If your students have computers at home, you can make a small pocket on the back of the book. Then place a disk with the slide show on it inside the pocket.

4. Arrange a slide show popcorn party where students to view their finished project.

5. Invite special guests, such as the principal, superintendent, and/or school nurse, to come to a special viewing of the slide show.

6. If your students are working in cooperative learning groups to make slide shows, you may wish to take group photos and scan them into the computer for use as the last slide in each group's show.

7. You may wish to have students record their names to tell who made the slide show. If you are putting together a class slide show, place each student's picture or drawing on one slide and scan in a school photograph for the next slide. Record each student saying, "By (student's name)."

Tips for Students

1. Encourage students to take advantage of using a lot of colors if you are not printing their slide show pictures.

2. Help students to be consistent in the colors, backgrounds, or frames they use so that the show is connected from slide to slide.

3. Help students be consistent with the placement of graphics or pictures within the slide show.

4. Have students vote to pick one font, font color, and font size for the entire slide show. Being consistent throughout the slide show will make it more professional looking.

5. Make sure the graphics and designs they add are meaningful to the slide.

6. Remind students that it is important for them to know when to stop. Point out that they should not let their pictures for the slide show get too busy.

7. If students are making a group slide show and you are recording their voices, you have two options. You can have students take turns recording so that you have a different group member's voice on each slide. As an alternative, you can record all the students in the group speaking together throughout the slide show.

Tips for Using Digital Photographs *(cont.)*

Tips for Using Digital Photographs

There are several ways to obtain digital photographs for use with computer software. Listed below are some suggestions.

1. Take photographs with a digital camera, download them to a disk, and import them into your software.

2. Scan a regular photograph, save the image to a disk, and import the photograph into your software.

3. Have the photographs developed and saved as a digital CD-ROM and import the pictures into your software. Ask about this option at your favorite photography developer. Some school photographers sell students' school pictures saved to CD-ROM.

4. Digital photographs can be imported into your software just as you would import any other picture or piece of clip art. Once the photograph is on the screen, you can resize it. Refer to the directions that came with your software for a more detailed explanation of this process.

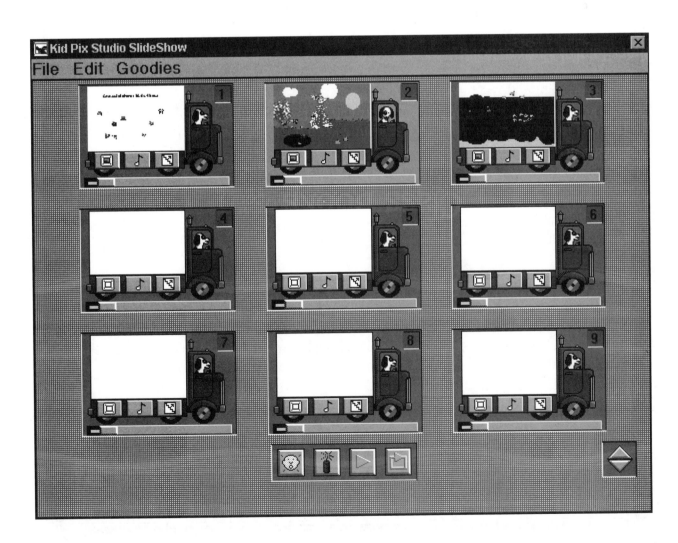

Outline of Projects

A The Absolutely Awesome Apostrophe Book, Acrostic Colors, Alphabet Avalanche, Alphabet Book, Animal Classification, Ant Art, Ant Math, Away with Arrays, Awesome Abe Lincoln (pages 15–23)

B Barnyard Counting Book, Barnyard Riddles, Bear Pictures, Beautiful Borders, Bodacious Bingo, Bookplates, Bow and Button Bonanza, Butterflies (pages 24–32)

C Calendars, The Very Hungry Caterpillar, Cinquain Poem, Class Flag, Collective Nouns, Compound Word Creations, Creepy Crawlies, Cultural Clothing (pages 33–40)

D Daytime/Nighttime, Design a Postage Stamp, Dominoes, Donut Fractions, Dot-to-Dot, Dynamic Dinosaurs (pages 41–46)

E Editing Excitement, Egg Book, Estimation Jar (pages 47–49)

F Fancy Facts, Fireworks Frenzy, Five Green and Speckled Frogs, Five Little Monkeys, Flat Stanley, Flowers (pages 50–55)

G Gingerbread Man, Gorgeous Gifts (pages 56 and 57)

H Happy Holidays, Healthy Meals, Homes and Addresses, How to Make 100 (page 58–61)

I Illustrating Poetry, In My Closet, Insect Counting Book, Insect Number Cubes Game, Interesting Insects, Invitations, Irresistible Iron-Ons (pages 62–68)

J Jack-O'-Lanterns, Jellybean Colors, Jellybean Counting, Jolly Jokes, Jovial Journal Covers, Jumpin' Jewels Game, Jumpin' Jewels Race (pages 69–75)

K The Very Hungry Kid, Kings and Queens (pages 76 and 77)

L Ladybug Math, Lemonade Signs, Lollipops (pages 78–80)

Outline of Projects *(cont.)*

M Marvelous Mittens, Me, Mix and Match, Monster Counting Book (pages 81–84)

N Nifty Names, Number Cubes Game, Number Cubes Magic, Number Word Match, Number Writing, I'm Nuts About... (pages 85-90)

O Ocean Pictures, Odd and Even, There Was an Old Lady Who Swallowed a Fly, Opposites (pages 91–94)

P Pairs, Patchwork Animal Slide Shows, Patterns, Penmanship, Perfect Postcards, Poetry Slide Shows, Polygons, Pop-Up Facts, Precise Punctuation, Pretty Pins, Puzzles (pages 95–105)

Q Quilts (page 106)

R Race from 100, Radical Riddles, Rebus Story, Rhyming (pages 107–110)

S Seasonal Hat, Secret Message, Shape Book, Shape-O-Rama, Shape Land, Spider Art, Spider Number Cubes Game, Spooky Stories, Stamp A Rainbow, Star Student, Stars (pages 111–121)

T Ten Apples Up On Top!, Book of Ten, Terrific Trees (pages 122–124)

U Under My Bed (page 125)

V Vacation Suitcases, Visits, Vowel Mobiles (pages 126–128)

W There's a Dragon in my Wagon, Wanted Posters, Watermelon Math, Web About Me, Web Buddies, Wild Things, Window Scenes, Wonderful Webs, Word-Processing Practice, Wrapping Paper (pages 129–138)

X X-cellent Equations (page 139)

Y Yellow Color Books, Yummy/Yucky (pages 140 and 141)

Z Zany Zoo (page 142)

Templates

Macintosh File Name	Windows File Name	Page Number	Macintosh File Name	Windows File Name	Page Number
Animal Classification	Animal.bmp	19	Number Cubes Magic	CubeMagi.bmp	87
Ant Math	AntMath.bmp	21	Number Word Match	NumMatch.bmp	88
Array	Array.bmp	22	I'm Nuts About…	Nuts.bmp	90
Barnyard Counting Book 1	Barn1.bmp	24	Odd/Even	OddEven.bmp	92
Barnyard Counting Book 2	Barn2.bmp	24	Old Lady	OldLady.bmp	93
Beautiful Border	Border.bmp	28	Patchwork Elephant	Elephant.bmp	96
Bodacious Bingo	Bingo.bmp	29	Polygon	Polygon.bmp	101
Bow and Button Bonanza	Bow.bmp	31	Race from 100	Race100.bmp	107
The Very Hungry Caterpillar	Caterpil.bmp	34	Seasons	Seasons.bmp	111
Cultural Clothing	Cultural.bmp	40	Circle	Circle.bmp	113
Daytime/Nighttime	DayNight.bmp	41	Rectangle	Rectangle.bmp	113
Domino 1	Domino1.bmp	43	Square	Square.bmp	113
Domino 2	Domino2.bmp	43	Triangle	Triangle.bmp	113
Estimation	Estimate.bmp	49	Spider Number Cubes Game	Spider.bmp	117
Gingerbread Man	Ginger.bmp	56	Star Student	StarStud.bmp	120
Gorgeous Gift	Gift.bmp	57	Stars	Stars.bmp	121
Holiday Chart	Holiday.bmp	58	Ten Apples Up On Top	TenApple.bmp	122
Apartment	Apt.bmp	60	Vacation Suitcase	Vacation.bmp	126
Home	Home.bmp	60	Vowel A, E, I	VowelAEI.bmp	128
Insect Counting Book 1	Insect1.bmp	64	Vowel O, U	VowelOU.bmp	128
Insect Counting Book 2	Insect2.bmp	64	Wagon	Wagon.bmp	129
Insect Number Cubes Game	InsGame.bmp	65	Watermelon	Watermel.bmp	131
Jack-O'-Lantern	Jack.bmp	69	Web About Me	WebAbtMe.bmp	132
Jellybean Colors	JelColor.bmp	70	Blue Color Book	Blue.bmp	140
Jellybean Counting	JelCount.bmp	71	Green Color Book	Green.bmp	140
Jumpin' Jewels	JumpJewl.bmp	74	Orange Color Book	Orange.bmp	140
Jumpin' Jewels Race	JumpRace.bmp	75	Purple Color Book	Purple.bmp	140
Ladybug Math 1	Ladybug1.bmp	78	Red Color Book	Red.bmp	140
Ladybug Math 2	Ladybug2.bmp	78	Yellow Color Book	Yellow.bmp	140
Marvelous Mittens	Mittens.bmp	81	Yummy/Yucky	YumYuck.bmp	141
Mix and Match	MixMatch.bmp	83	Zany Zoo	ZanyZoo.bmp	142
Number Cubes Game	CubeGame.bmp	86			

The Absolutely Awesome Apostrophe Book

Software
- Any word processor

Skills Developed
- Apostrophes
- Reading
- Contractions
- Creative writing

Materials
- Chart paper
- Markers
- String or yarn
- Cardstock
- Cellophane tape

Template
- No template is needed.

Before the Computer
1. As a class, brainstorm a list of contractions and write them on a piece of chart paper.
2. Hang the chart near the computers.
3. Prior to beginning the project, specify the font, font size, and font style that you want students to use.

At the Computer
1. Open the word processor.
2. Type a sentence using a large font size. Use two or more contractions in the sentence and leave out the apostrophes.
3. Print.
4. Cut off any excess paper.

After the Computer
1. Put the pages with the sentences together to make a class book.
2. Write an apostrophe on a small rectangle cut from cardstock.
3. Tape one end of a piece of string or yarn to the back of the cardstock with the apostrophe on it. Tie the other end of the string or yarn onto the top left-hand binding of the book.
4. Allow each student to read through the book and place the apostrophe where it is needed in each contraction.
5. Students can take turns taking this book home to share with their families.

Acrostic Colors

Software

- Any drawing software that includes stamps

Skills Developed

- Reading and spelling color words
- Use of stamps

Materials

- No additional materials are needed.

Template

- No template is needed.

Before the Computer

- No introductory activities are needed.

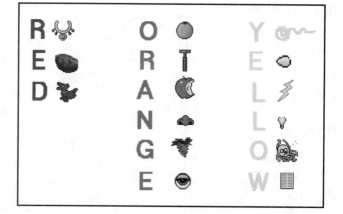

At the Computer

1. Open the drawing software.
2. Select a color, and type the name of that color vertically on the screen.
3. Place a stamp next to each letter. The name of the picture stamped should begin with that letter and it should also be that color. See the examples shown above. Some letters may be difficult to match with stamps. Draw pictures for these, or if the existing stamps can be edited, change the color of the stamps to go with the different letters.
4. Change colors and color words and repeat the procedure with each new color name.
5. Print.

After the Computer

1. You can make a rainbow display of your acrostic colors. In the order of colors in a rainbow, vertically hang strips of red, orange, yellow, green, blue, indigo, and violet colored butcher paper on a wall.
2. Arrange the acrostic color pictures on the rainbow background.

Alphabet Avalanche

Software
- Any drawing software that includes stamps and allows you to add text

Skills Developed
- Letter-sound recognition
- Use of stamps

Materials
- Alphabet chart

Template
- No template is needed.

Before the Computer
- Post the alphabet chart near the computers.

At the Computer
1. Open the drawing software.
2. Type the letters **Aa** at the top left-hand corner of the screen.
3. Find a stamp with a picture name that begins with the either the uppercase **A** or lowercase **a**. Stamp it underneath the letters. If you cannot find a stamp with a picture name that begins with **A** or **a**, draw a picture of something with a name that begins with **A** or **a** under the letters.
4. Next, type the letters **Bb**.
5. Find a stamp with a picture name that begins with either the uppercase **B** or lowercase **b**. Stamp it underneath the letters. If you cannot find a stamp with a picture name that begins with **B** or **b**, draw a picture of something with a name that begins with **B** or **b** under the letters.
6. Continue typing all the letters of the alphabet and adding the appropriate stamps or drawings underneath each one.
7. Print or check.

Aa	Bb	Cc	Dd	Ee	Ff	Gg	Hh

Alphabet Book

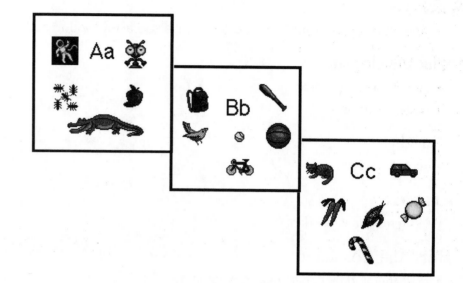

Software

- Any drawing software that includes stamps

Skills Developed

- Letter recognition
- Letter-sound recognition
- Use of stamps

Materials

- No additional materials are needed.

Template

- No template is needed.

Before the Computer

1. Tell students that you are going to make a class alphabet book. Assign a letter of the alphabet to each child.
2. If you have fewer than 26 students in your class, it can be fun to ask school personnel, such as the principal, secretary, and nurse, to make a page. You can make a page, too.
3. Note: It is very difficult to find stamps for some letters. Tell students to draw pictures for those letters. For letter **X**, have them stamp **X**s, and for letter **Y**, they can use stamps that are yellow.

At the Computer

1. Open the drawing software.
2. Type your assigned letter at the top of the screen.
3. Choose the stamp tool and stamp as many things as you can find whose names begin with that letter.
4. Remember that if you can't find stamps for your letter, you can draw pictures whose names begin with that letter.
5. Print.

After the Computer

1. Put the pages together to make an alphabet book.
2. You can let the children check out the class book to take home and share with their families, or you can make photocopies of the book so each child has a copy to keep.

Variation

- Have each student make his/her own alphabet book.

Animal Classification

Software

- Any drawing software that includes a variety of animal stamps

Skills Developed

- Fine motor
- Animal classification
- Use of stamps
- Brainstorming ideas
- Use of an idea web

Materials

- Chart paper
- Markers

Template

- Animal Classification Template

Before the Computer

1. Discuss which animals can be classified in each category (Mammals, Birds, Reptiles, Amphibians, Fish) and brainstorm a list of them.
2. Write the list on chart paper.

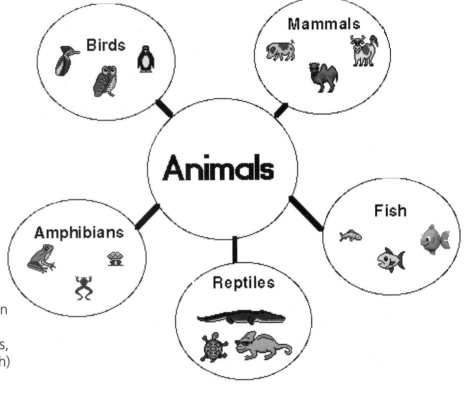

At the Computer

1. Open the drawing software.
2. Find the Animal Classification Template on the CD-ROM and import it into your drawing software.
3. Choose the stamp tool and stamp things that fit into each of the animal categories. If stamps for some of the categories are not available, you can draw your own animal pictures.
4. Print.

Ant Art

Software
- Any drawing software

Skills Developed
- Counting
- Drawing
- Knowledge of insects

Materials
- No additional materials are needed.

Template
- No template is needed.

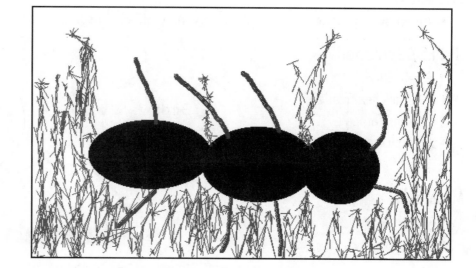

Before the Computer
- Talk about the characteristics of insects, including that they have three body parts, two eyes, two antennae, and six legs.

At the Computer
1. Open the drawing software.
2. Use your drawing tools to draw the body of an ant. If you have a circle tool, you can use it to make the three body parts of the ant.
3. Use your drawing tools to draw six legs on the ant.
4. Add any other details to make the ant look realistic.
5. You may wish to draw scenery as a background for the ant.
6. Print.

Extended Activities
- For added practice with math skills, you can click on the A tool and use the numbers to stamp 3 + 3 = 6 to go along with the ant's legs.

Ant Math

Software

- Any drawing software that has a stamp of an ant

Skills Developed

- Number recognition
- Counting

Materials

- No additional materials are needed.

Template

- Ant Math Template

Before the Computer

- No introductory activities are needed.

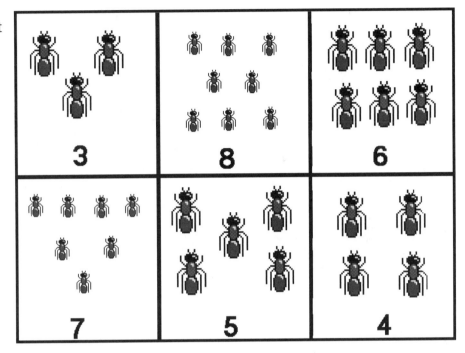

At the Computer

1. Open the drawing software.
2. Find the Ant Math Template on the CD-ROM and import it into your drawing software.
3. Select the stamp tool and find the stamp of an ant.
4. Stamp the correct number of ants in each section.
5. Print.

Variation

- You can use a different stamp to go with a particular holiday or the unit you are studying. Examples: On Halloween you can do Pumpkin Math and have students use the pumpkin stamp. On Valentine's Day you can do Heart Math and have students use the heart stamp. For a unit about food, you can do Food Math and have students use food stamps.

Away With Arrays

Software
- Kid Pix

Skills Developed
- Multiplication facts

Materials
- No additional materials are needed.

Template
- Array Template

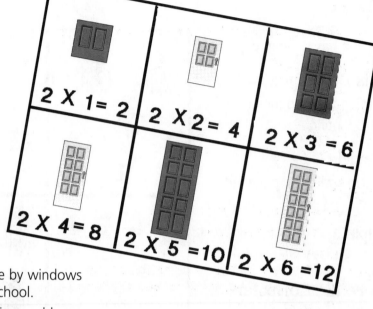

Before the Computer

1. Point out arrays, such as those made by windows and bricks, which are part of your school.
2. Compare each array to a multiplication problem.

At the Computer

1. Open Kid Pix.
2. Open the Array Template on the CD-ROM.
3. Choose the Wacky Paintbrush tool and go to the Build a House option at the bottom of the screen.
4. Select any of the choices that will build any part of the house that has an array, such as the brown door. Click and drag an array into each section of the Array Template.
5. Use the Talking Alphabet Stamps tool to make a multiplication equation for each array.
6. Use the capital letter X for the multiplication sign.

Extended Activities

- You can designate a number of vertical columns to make in each array. Each of the arrays in the sections of the template can have a different number of vertical columns. This can help illustrate multiplication facts for beginners.

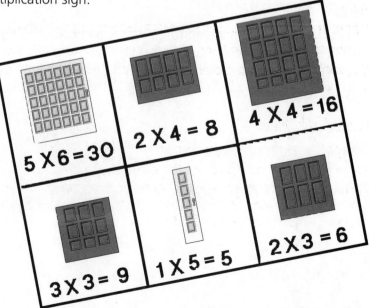

Awesome Abe Lincoln

Software

- Any drawing software that allows you to add text

Skills Developed

- Drawing
- Reading
- Fine motor
- Creative writing

Materials

- School photograph of each student
- Books about Abraham Lincoln

  Suggestions:
  Abe Lincoln's Hat by Martha Brenner (Random, 1994)
  Abraham Lincoln: A Photo-Illustrated Biography by T.M. Usel (Carlton Press, 1996)
  Honest Abe by Edith Kunhardt (Greenwillow, 1993)

If I were president, I would...

Template

- No template is needed.

Before the Computer

- Read a story about Abraham Lincoln and discuss the responsibilities that a president has.

At the Computer

1. Open the drawing software.
2. Import or copy and paste your photograph into the drawing software.
3. Use the drawing tools to add details to your picture such as a beard and a tall hat.
4. Type a sentence about what you might do if you were president or if you were Abraham Lincoln.
5. Print.

Extended Activities

1. These pictures make a great display for Presidents' Day.
2. You might also want to save all of students' creations in a special folder and later put them into a slide show. Students can record their voices telling what they would do if they were president or if they were Abraham Lincoln. Then you can assemble the slide show so that the students' voices can be heard when their pictures are shown.

Barnyard Counting Book

Software
- Any drawing software that includes stamps and allows you to add text

Skills Developed
- Recognition of barnyard animals
- Counting

Materials
- Chart paper   • Marker
- Stapler or yarn and a hole puncher

Templates
- Barnyard Counting Book 1 Template
- Barnyard Counting Book 2 Template

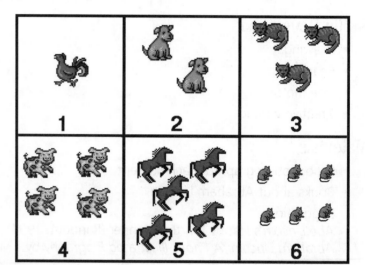

Before the Computer
1. As a class, brainstorm a list of animals that you might find on a farm.
2. List these animals on a piece of chart paper.
3. Display the chart near the computers.

At the Computer
1. Open the drawing software.
2. Find the Barnyard Counting Book 1 Template on the CD-ROM and import it into your drawing software.
3. Select the stamp tool and find a stamp of an animal that might be found on a farm. Note that the number 1 is in the first section. Stamp the animal one time in the first section to go with the number 1.
4. Find a different barnyard animal stamp for each section. Stamp the appropriate number of animals to go with the number in each section.
5. Print.
6. Repeat this procedure with the Barnyard Counting Book 2 Template.

After the Computer
1. Cut off any excess paper.
2. Cut each page apart along the lines.
3. Staple the book together or punch two holes and bind the book with yarn bows.

Variation
- You can use stamps to go along with any unit you are studying. Examples: If you are studying the rainforest, have students make a Rainforest Counting Book. If you are studying about Christmas, you can have students make a Gingerbread Man Counting Book.

Barnyard Riddles

Software

- Any drawing software that includes stamps and allows you to add text

Skills Developed

- Recognition of barnyard animals
- Reading

Materials

- Chart paper
- Markers
- Glue
- White construction paper
- Scissors
- Barn pattern reproduced on red copier paper (one per child; one for the cover)

Template

- No template is needed.

Before the Computer

1. As a class, brainstorm a list of animals and things that you might find on a farm.
2. Write these animals on a chart.
3. Have each student sign up to make a riddle for one of the animals listed.

At the Computer

1. Open the drawing software.
2. Stamp your barnyard animal in the middle of the page.
3. Type the question: What goes _____ , _____? Fill in the blanks with an animal sound. For example, your question might read, "What goes quack, quack?"
4. Type the name of the animal (a _____) at the bottom of the page. For example, if you used the question shown in step 3, you would type "a duck."
5. If your software gives you an option to change the size of the picture, print a medium-sized picture.
6. Cut out a red barn. Cut along the dotted line between the barn doors. Then fold the barn doors open. Glue the barn onto a 9" x 11" (23 cm x 28 cm) piece of white construction paper, making sure you do not glue down the barn doors.
7. Cut out the picture of the barnyard animal that you stamped. Glue the animal inside the barn doors.
8. Then cut out the question you typed, and glue it at the top of the page.
9. Finally, cut out the name of the animal and glue it inside the barn doors, under the picture.

After the Computer

1. This can be made into a class book.
2. The children can take it home to share with their families.

Barnyard Riddles Pattern

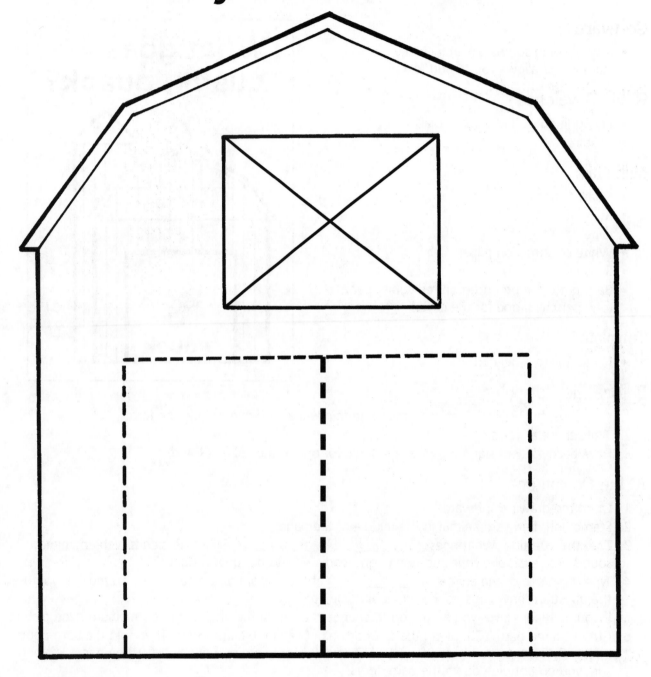

Bear Pictures

Software

- Any drawing software

Skills Developed

- Drawing
- Fine motor

Materials

- Books about real bears
  Suggestions:
  Bears by Bobbie Kalman
  (Crabtree, 1994)
  Bears by Helen Gilks
  (Houghton Mifflin, 1993)
  Bears in the Forest by Karen
  Wallace (Candlewick Press, 1994)

Template

- No template is needed.

Before the Computer

1. Provide a variety of books about real bears for students to enjoy.
2. Allow time for students to look at the books so that they can see pictures of real bears in their natural habitats.

At the Computer

1. Open the drawing software.
2. Use your drawing tools to make a picture of a bear. Make it look as real as you can. Add details such as fur, ears, and a tail. If your drawing software has a circle tool available, you can use it to make the bear's head and body.
3. Create a realistic habitat for your bear by drawing scenery around him.
4. Print.

After the Computer

1. The bear pictures can be made into a class book.
2. Students can take the book home to share with their families.

Beautiful Borders

Software
- Any drawing software with stamps available

Skills Developed
- Drawing
- Fine motor

Materials
- Scissors
- Stapler
- Cotton balls
- Colored glue (optional)

Template
- Beautiful Border Template

Before the Computer
- No introductory activities are needed.

At the Computer
1. Open the drawing software.
2. Find the Beautiful Border Template on the CD-ROM and import it into your drawing software.
3. Select stamps that go with the theme, unit, holiday, or season you are studying. Stamp a pattern across the first row. Then continue to stamp the same pattern in the following rows.
4. Use different drawing tools to add designs and details to your pattern as seen in the examples at the bottom of this page.
5. Print several copies.

After the Computer
- Cut along the lines and staple the borders around a bulletin board or display.

Extended Activities
1. You can make your borders 3-dimensional by adding your favorite craft supplies.
2. Try pulling apart cotton balls and attaching them as clouds.
3. You can also add colorful accents with colored glue.

Bodacious Bingo

Software

- Any drawing software that includes stamps

Skills Developed

- Listening
- Fine motor

Materials

- Scissors
- Bingo markers or buttons
- Jar

Template

- Bodacious Bingo Template

Before the Computer

1. Choose a set of stamps for students to use to make bingo cards. You may wish to pick a set of stamps that relate to a specific theme or holiday that you are studying.
2. Make a master copy of all the stamps by stamping each one in that set on a blank screen.
3. Print and cut them apart.

At the Computer

1. Open the drawing software.
2. Find the Grid Template on the CD-ROM and import it into your drawing software.
3. Find the set of stamps selected by your teacher. Make a bingo card by stamping a different stamp in each of the boxes. Be sure you use each stamp only one time.
4. Print.

After the Computer

1. To play bingo, put the stamps that you have cut apart in a jar.
2. Designate whether students must have one row or the entire bingo card covered to win the game.
3. Pull out one picture at a time, and call out the name of that picture.
4. As you call out the picture names, have students cover the pictures on their bingo cards with bingo markers or buttons.
5. After playing, save the bingo cards and jar of pictures so the class can play over and over again.

Variation

- You may wish to allow a group of students to play bingo rather than involving the whole class.

Bookplates

Software
- Any drawing software that allows you to add text

Skills Developed
- Drawing
- Word processing
- Fine motor

Materials
- Scissors
- Glue stick

Templates
- No template is needed.

Before the Computer
- No introductory activities are needed.

This book belongs to:

At the Computer
1. Open the drawing software.
2. Type the following sentence: This book belongs to _____. Type your name in the blank. Example: This book belongs to John.
3. Use the drawing tools and stamps to create a unique book plate. Make your book plate small enough to fit on the inside cover of your books.
4. Print several copies of your bookplate for your books.

After the Computer
1. Cut off any excess paper.
2. Use a glue stick to glue one bookplate onto the inside cover of each book.

Extended Activities
1. These bookplates make great gifts for the holidays.
2. Teachers can make special bookplates that read, "This book was donated by _____ ," for students who donate books to the class.

Bow and Button Bonanza

Software
- *Kid Pix*

Skills Developed
- Addition
- Use of a calculator

Materials
- One calculator per student

Template
- Bow and Button Bonanza Template

Before the Computer
- Allow students some free time to explore the calculators.

✦	1	$3 + 8 + 6 + 1 + 2 + 7 = 27$
●	2	
✦	3	$6 + 5 + 8 + 7 + 1 + 2 = 29$
●	4	
✿	5	$2 + 5 + 1 + 8 + 4 + 6 + 3 + 1 = 30$
●	6	
❀	7	$7 + 4 + 3 + 5 + 2 = 21$
✦	8	

At the Computer
1. Open *Kid Pix.*
2. Find the Bow and Button Bonanza Template on the CD-ROM and import it into Kid Pix.
3. Choose the Wacky Paintbrush tool. Select the yellow bow with the purple background.
4. Drag a row of bows into each empty section.
5. Use the Talking Alphabet Stamps tool to make addition equations that go with each row. Refer to the key for the value of each picture.
6. Use a calculator to add all of the numbers in each row.
7. Use the Talking Alphabet Stamps tool to write the sum, or total, at the end of each row.
8. Print or check.
9. This game can be played over and over again for more addition practice and fun with calculators.

Butterflies

Software
- Any drawing software such as *Kid Works*

Skills Developed
- Fine motor
- Use of drawing tools
- Symmetry

Materials
- Yarn (optional)

Template
- No template is needed.

Before the Computer
- No introductory activities are needed.

At the Computer
1. Open the drawing software.
2. Use any drawing tools to create a picture of a butterfly. Remember that if you draw a butterfly, the wing colors and patterns must match each other. **Note:** If you are using *Kid Works*, you can select the mirror tool before you draw. This tool will make a mirror image of whatever you draw.
3. Print.

Extended Activity
- You can make and print out several butterflies. Then hang them on pieces of yarn to make a mobile.

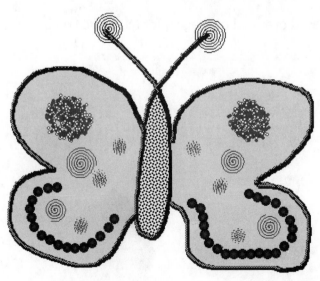

Calendars

Software

- Any software that allows you to make a calendar

Skills Developed

- Use of calendars
- Recognition of holidays and special dates

Materials

- Chart paper
- Markers

Template

- No template is needed.

🍎 September 🍎

Sunday	Monday	Tuesday	Wednesday	Thursday	Friday	Saturday
	1	2	3	4	5	6
7	8	9	10	11	12	13
14	15	16	17	18	19	20
21	22	23	24	25	26	27
28	29	30				

Before the Computer

1. Brainstorm a list of holidays and special dates that are in each month.
2. List them on a piece of chart paper.

At the Computer

1. Open the calendar software.
2. If your software gives you different calendar options, choose the type of calendar you would like to make.
3. Choose the correct month and year.
4. Type in the names of any holidays and special dates for that month.
5. Print.

Variations

1. As an alternative to making one calendar each month, you may wish to have students make a calendar for the entire year.
2. For younger students, you may wish to type in the names of the special days for them. Then have students make illustrations to go with the special days in each month.

The Very Hungry Caterpillar

Software
- Any drawing software that allows you to add text

Skills Developed
- Listening
- Creative writing

Materials
- *The Very Hungry Caterpillar* by Eric Carle (Philomel, 1969)

Template
- The Very Hungry Caterpillar Template

Before the Computer
- Read aloud *The Very Hungry Caterpillar* by Eric Carle to students.

At the Computer
1. Open the drawing software.
2. Find The Very Hungry Caterpillar Template on the CD-ROM and import it into your drawing software.
3. Stamp something next to the caterpillar that you would like the hungry caterpillar to eat.
4. Type the name of the food that you stamped to complete the sentence. Then type your name.
5. Print.

After the Computer
1. You can make a class book with these pictures.
2. Have students take the book home to share with their families. Send home the class-made book with a copy of *The Very Hungry Caterpillar* by Eric Carle in a resealable plastic bag.

Cinquain Poem

Software

- Any software that includes stamps and allows you to add text

Skills Developed

- Creative writing
- Vocabulary development
- Drawing

Materials

- No additional materials are needed.

Template

- No template is needed.

Before the Computer

1. Discuss the following Cinquain format with your students.

   Line 1: One-word title
   Line 2: Two words that describe the title
   Line 3: Three words that describe an action
   Line 4: Four words that describe a feeling
   Line 5: Another word for the title

2. Brainstorm topics for Cinquain poems.

At the Computer

1. Open the drawing software.
2. Create and type a Cinquain poem.
3. Add illustrations and/or stamps around the text that relate to the poem.
4. Print.

After the Computer

1. These poems can be displayed in class or put into a class book for students to take home to share with their families.
2. If you are making a class book, you may wish to type a copy of the Cinquain poem format, as shown above in Before the Computer, and add it to the beginning of the book.

Class Flags

Software

- Any drawing software

Skills Developed

- Drawing
- Fine motor

Materials

- Books with pictures of flags from different countries and/or states

Suggestions:

- *Flag* by William Crampton (Alfred A. Knopf, 1989)
- *Flags* by Chris Oxlade (Franklin Watts, 1995)
- *State Flags* by Sue R. Brandt (Franklin Watts, 1992)

Template

- No template is needed.

Before the Computer

1. Have a variety of books with pictures of flags in them for students to preview.
2. Have students look for colors and patterns in different flags.

At the Computer

1. Open the drawing software.
2. Use your drawing tools, stamps, and graphics to design a flag. Make sure the colors and graphics that you use have a purpose. Do not make your flag too busy.
3. Print.

Extended Activities

- Display the flags somewhere in the classroom. Have students vote to select their favorite flag. Use the flag that gets the most votes as the "Class Flag."

Collective Nouns

Software
- Any drawing software that allows you to add text

Skills Developed
- Listening
- Drawing
- Word processing
- Creative writing

Materials
- *A Cache of Jewels and Other Collective Nouns* by Ruth Heller (Grosset, 1987)
- Chart paper
- Marker

Template
- No template is needed.

A school of fish swim around.

Before the Computer
1. Read *A Cache of Jewels and Other Collective Nouns* by Ruth Heller.
2. Brainstorm a list of collective nouns. Students can feel free to use the collective nouns mentioned in the book and they can come up with their own as well.
3. Write the list of collective nouns on chart paper. Have each student sign up for a collective noun.
4. Ask students to use their collective nouns in sentences and illustrate their sentences.

At the Computer
1. Open the drawing software.
2. Think of a sentence that uses your collective noun.
3. Type your sentence at the top of the screen.
3. Use the drawing tools to illustrate your sentence.
4. Print.

After the Computer
1. You can put the pictures together into a class book.
2. Have students take the book home to share with their families. Send home the class-made book with a copy of *A Cache of Jewels and Other Collective Nouns* by Ruth Heller in a resealable plastic bag.

Compound Word Creations

Software
- Any drawing software with stamps that allows you to add text

Skills Developed
- Brainstorming ideas
- Drawing
- Compound words
- Vocabulary development

Materials
- Chart paper
- Markers

Template
- No template is needed.

Before the Computer
1. Discuss what a compound word is.
2. Have students name compound words they know.
3. List the compound words on a piece of chart paper.
4. Hang the chart paper near the computers.
5. You may wish to assign partners or cooperative learning groups for this activity.

At the Computer
1. Open the drawing software.
2. Use stamps or draw your own illustrations to create pictures that demonstrate the literal meaning of the compound words.
3. Type the compound word next to each picture.
4. Print.

After the Computer
- Display the pictures on a bulletin board entitled "Compound Word Creations."

Creepy Crawlies

Software
- Any drawing software that allows you to add text

Skills Developed
- Drawing
- Creative writing
- Identification of insects

Materials
- No additional materials are needed.

Template
- No template is needed.

Before the Computer
1. Tell students to pretend that they can change into insects, or creepy crawlies.
2. Ask them what creepy crawlies they would like to be.

At the Computer
1. Open a drawing software.
2. Use your drawing tools to make a picture of the creepy crawly you would like to be.
3. Type the following sentence: If I could be a creepy crawly, I would be a(n) _____ because I like _____ .
4. Print.

After the Computer
1. These pages can be made into a class book.
2. Allow students to take the book home to share with their families.

If I could be a creepy crawly, I would be a ladybug because I like the color red.

Cultural Clothing

Software
- Any software that includes stamps and allows you to add text

Skills Developed
- Recognition of different cultures
- Drawing
- Fine motor

Hawaii, USA

Materials
- Chart paper
- Markers
- Books about clothing from different countries

Suggestions:
- *Costumes and Clothes* (Marshall Cavendish, 1989)
- *Folk & Festival Costumes of the World* by Riturner Wilcox (Charles Scribner's Sons, 1965)
- *Hats, Hats, Hats* by Ann Morris (Lothrop, 1989)
- *Uncle Nacho's Hat* by Harriet Rohmer and Rosalma Zubizarreta (Childrens Press, 1989)

Template
- Cultural Clothing Template

Before the Computer
1. Discuss the different types of traditional clothing that are worn in foreign countries. Show pictures of clothing from a variety of books.
2. On a piece of chart paper, list the names of some of the countries for which traditional clothing is shown in the books.
3. Have each student sign up for a country on the list.
4. Ask students to make a picture on the computer of their country's traditional clothing.

At the Computer
1. Open the drawing software.
2. Find the Cultural Clothing Template on the CD-ROM and import it into your drawing software.
3. Use the drawing tools and stamps to decorate and add details to the template.
4. Type the name of the country above your picture.
5. Print.

Extended Activities
1. You can display the clothing on a bulletin board entitled "Clothing from Different Cultures." Place a world map in the center of the bulletin board. Use yarn to connect each type of traditional clothing with its country of origin.
2. You can cut out the clothing and allow students to use it on paper dolls.

Daytime/Nighttime

Software

- Any drawing software that includes stamps

Skills Developed

- Use of stamps
- Sorting

Materials

- No additional materials are needed.

Template

- Daytime/Nighttime Template

Before the Computer

- Talk about things that you might see in the daytime and other things that you might see in the nighttime.

At the Computer

1. Open the drawing software.
2. Find the Daytime/Nighttime Template on the CD-ROM and import it into your drawing software.
3. Choose stamps of things that you might see in the daytime. Stamp those pictures under the daytime heading.
4. Choose stamps of things that you might see in the nighttime. Stamp those pictures under the nighttime heading.
5. Print.

Extended Activities

1. Discuss how the rotation of the Earth causes daytime and nighttime.
2. Explain to students that one half of the Earth is having daytime while the other half is having nighttime.

Design a Postage Stamp

Software
- Any drawing software that allows you to add text

Skills Developed
- Drawing
- Fine motor

Materials
- Pinking shears or any brand of zigzag scissors
- A variety of postage stamps
- Magnifying glasses

Template
- No template is needed.

Before the Computer
- Provide magnifying glasses and a variety of postage stamps for students to examine some different stamp designs.

At the Computer
1. Open your drawing software.
2. Use your drawing tools to make a small rectangle. The rectangle should be larger than a regular postage stamp so that you have room to draw inside of it.
3. Create a new design for a postage stamp and draw it inside your rectangle.
4. Select a small font and type USA and the value of the stamp.
5. Print.

After the Computer
- Cut out your stamp using pinking shears or any scissors that cut with a zigzag edge. Be sure to leave a 1/8'' (0.3 cm) border of white around the outer edge.

Extended Activities
- Discuss how stamps are usually designed to show famous people or special events. Students can design their stamps to show something that is important to them. Then ask them to write or tell about the significance of their designs.

Dominoes

Software
- Any drawing software that allows you to add text

Skills Developed
- Number recognition
- Counting
- Addition
- Subtraction

Materials
- No additional materials are needed.

Templates
- Domino 1 Template
- Domino 2 Template

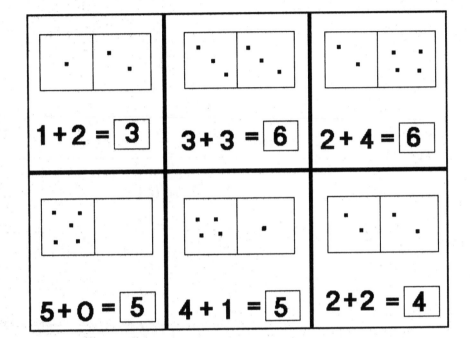

Before the Computer
- No introductory activities are needed.

At the Computer
1. Open the drawing software.
2. Find Domino 1 Template on the CD-ROM and import it into your drawing software.
3. Use your drawing tools to add dots on the dominoes to match the equations.
4. Type the sum at the end of each equation in the box provided.
5. Print or check.
6. Open Domino 2 Template.
7. Type equations to match the dots on each domino.
8. Print or check.

Extended Activity
- For an added challenge, add dots and stamp numbers to complete subtraction equations.

Donut Fractions

Software
- Any drawing software

Skills Developed
- Fractions
- Drawing
- Fine motor

Materials
- *Eating Fractions* by Bruce McMillan (Scholastic, 1992)
- Five 8.5" x 11" (22 cm x 28 cm) pieces of construction paper for each student
- Scissors
- Glue sticks
- Pencils
- Stapler

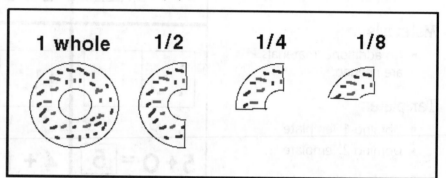

Template
- No template is needed.

Before the Computer
- Read *Eating Fractions* by Bruce McMillan.

At the Computer
1. Open the drawing software.
2. Use the circle tool or any other drawing tools to make a large donut.
3. Use painting tools to fill in your donut and add sprinkles, nuts, etc.
4. Print two full-size copies of your donut.

After the Computer
1. Cut off the excess white paper from both donuts.
2. Glue one whole donut onto a piece of construction paper. Write "1 whole" at the top.
3. Fold the second donut in half, and cut it along the fold line.
4. Glue ½ of the donut onto a blank piece of construction paper. Write "½" at the top.
5. Fold the remaining ½ of the donut in half again. Cut along the fold line, making ²/₄.
6. Glue ¼ onto a blank piece of construction paper. Write "¼" at the top of this paper.
7. Fold the remaining ¼ in half again. Cut along the fold line, making ²/₈.
8. Glue ⅛ of the donut onto a blank piece of construction paper. Write "⅛" at the top.
9. Make a cover page entitled "My Donut Fraction Book" by _____ . Write your name in the blank.
10. Glue the remaining ⅛ piece of donut on the cover for decoration.
11. Staple the fraction book together.

Dot-to-Dot

Software
- *Kid Pix*

Skills Developed
- Number recognition
- Counting
- Fine motor

Materials
- Laminating film and laminator or clear contact paper (optional)
- Wipe-off crayons or wipe-off markers (optional)

Template
- No template is needed.

Before the Computer
- No introductory activities are needed.

At the Computer
1. Open *Kid Pix*.
2. Choose the Wacky Paintbrush tool and the Dot-to-Dot option at the bottom of the screen. This will look like 1-2-3 with dots and lines. It is on the third level, in the first box on the left.
3. Make a random dot-to-dot by dragging the paintbrush across the screen. Be careful not to overlap the dots and numbers.
4. Choose the stamp tool for a small star or another small stamp. Stamp that picture next to the first dot and next to the last dot.
5. Then type the word "Start" by number one and "Finish" by the last number.
6. Print.

Variations
1. Allow students to make several copies of their dot-to-dots to trade with their friends.
2. Laminate the dot-to-dots so that they are reusable. Allow students to draw on them with wipe-off crayons or markers.
3. Another option is to leave the dot-to-dot on the screen and have students use the line tool to complete the picture.

Dynamic Dinosaurs

Software
- *Kid Pix*

Skills Developed
- Drawing
- Reading
- Spelling
- Fine motor
- Knowledge of dinosaur names

Materials
- Chart paper
- Marker

Template
- No template is needed.

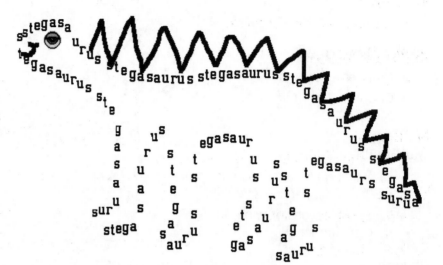

Before the Computer
1. Have students brainstorm a list of dinosaur names.
2. Write the list on the chart paper.
3. Assign a dinosaur to each student or allow each student to pick a dinosaur.

At the Computer
1. Open *Kid Pix*.
2. Go to the Talking Alphabet tool under the TOOLBOX menu.
3. Type the name of your dinosaur over and over with a space in between each name until you get to the end of the line and click OK.
4. Select the Wacky Paintbrush tool from the tool bar and choose the Alphabet Line option (ABC) at the bottom of the screen.
5. To draw your dinosaur, click and hold down the mouse. Then drag the paintbrush across the screen.
6. Use the drawing tools and stamps to add details such as eyes, claws, teeth, and bony plates to your dinosaur.
7. Print.

Extended Activities
1. Add a prehistoric background to the dinosaurs before you print.
2. As an alternative to the above activity, have students cut out the dinosaurs and display them in a prehistoric scene made on a bulletin board or wall.

Editing Excitement

Software
- Any word-processing software

Skills Developed
- Word processing
- Editing

Materials
- No additional materials are needed.

Template
- No template is needed.

> The *quick* brown <u>fox</u> jumped **OVER** the lazy **dog**.

Before the Computer
1. Open the word-processing software.
2. Type the following sentence in a large font: "The quick brown fox jumped over the lazy dog."
3. Save this sentence for your students, and entitle it "Editing Excitement."

At the Computer
1. Open the word-processing software. Open "Editing Excitement."
2. Change the font, styles, and sizes of specified words according to your teacher's instructions. Here are some examples:

    Change the word "quick" to Italics.
    Underline the word "fox."
    Change the size of the word "jumped" to 18 pt.
    Choose a new font for the word "over."
    Change the word "dog" to bold.

3. Print or check.

Extended Activity
- You can choose different students to give the oral instructions on how to change the words in the sentence. Then your students will be experts for when they edit their own stories.

Egg Book

Software

- Any drawing software that includes stamps and allows you to add text

Skills Developed

- Knowledge of which animals hatch from eggs
- Reading

Materials

- Manila paper
- Scissors
- Glue

Template

- No template is needed.

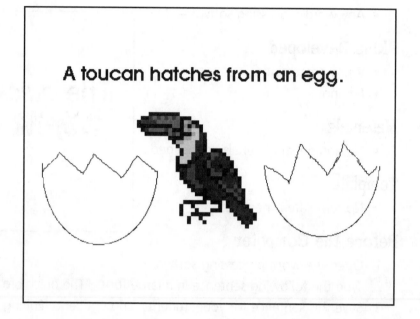

A toucan hatches from an egg.

Before the Computer

1. Brainstorm a list of living things that hatch from eggs.
2. Have each student sign up to make a picture of one of these living things on the computer.

At the Computer

1. Open the drawing software.
2. Stamp or draw the animal that hatches from an egg.
3. Type the following sentence: A(n) _____ hatches from an egg. Type the name of the animal in the blank.
4. Print.

After the Computer

1. These pictures can be put into a class book.
2. Encourage students to take the book home to share with their families.

Extended Activity

- You can cut cracked eggs out of Manila paper. If you have a die-cut machine at your school, there may be a cracked egg pattern available. Glue a cracked egg opening up on each page. Have students glue their animal pictures coming out of the cracked eggs.

Estimation Jar

Software
- Any drawing software with stamps

Skills Developed
- Number recognition
- Estimation
- Counting

Materials
- Clear plastic or glass jar
- Any small items that can be used for estimating
- Chart Paper to record estimates
- Markers

Template
- Estimation Template

How many <u>bear counters</u> are there?

There are <u>25 bear counters</u>.

Before the Computer
This is to be completed by the teacher prior to the lesson.

1. Open your drawing program.
2. Find the Estimation Template on the CD-ROM and import it into your drawing program.
3. Find a stamp of the item you are estimating in the jar and stamp it several times in the jar on the screen. If you do not have a stamp of the item you are estimating, you can draw it and copy and paste it several times in the jar.

Note: You are not stamping the exact number of pictures to equal the amount in the jar. The amount stamped is just a representation of the actual amount.

4. Using a color other than black, complete the sentences. Leave a blank spot for the amount.
5. If you have a computer available in your classroom, leave this on the screen for the activity. Otherwise, print the page and bring it to your classroom.

At the Computer:
This is to be done by the whole class.

1. Allow each student to guess how many items are in the jar and record their estimations.
2. Count out items by 10s, 5s, or 2s as a class.
3. Discuss if the estimates on the chart paper were too large or too small. Do not point out whose estimate was whose in order to avoid hurt feelings.
4. Choose a student to type the correct amount in the blank on the computer. If you do not have a computer in class, have a student write the amount with a marker on the printed page.
5. Print.

After the Computer
- Throughout the year, save different estimation pages that you do with the class. These estimation pages can be put in a class book for the students to take home and share with their families.

Fancy Facts

Software

- Any software that allows you to make customized greeting cards

Skills Developed

- Reading
- Word processing
- Vocabulary development

Materials

- Chart paper
- Markers

Template

- No template is needed.

Before the Computer

1. As a class, brainstorm a list of facts that you know about a topic you are studying. For example, if you are studying bears, you might list the following: Bears are mammals. Bears hibernate in the winter. Bears eat berries and fish.
2. Assign a fact to each student.

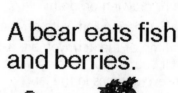

At the Computer

1. Open the greeting card software.
2. Type a question about your fact on the cover of the card. Example: What do bears eat?
3. Add stamps, drawings, or borders to the front of your card if they relate to your question.
4. Go to the inside of the card, and type the answer to the question using a complete sentence. Example: A bear eats berries and fish.
5. Add any appropriate pictures, drawings, or borders to the inside of the card.
6. Print.
7. Fold the print-out into a card.

After the Computer

1. Make a 3-dimensional display of your questions and facts by attaching them to a bulletin board or wall. Be sure to display the cards at a height that children can reach so they can peek inside to see the answers to the questions.
2. Use a title such as "Fancy Facts about Bears."

Fireworks Frenzy

Software
- *Kid Pix*

Skills Developed
- Fine motor
- Drawing
- Knowledge of paintbrush tools
- Recognition of the Fourth of July holiday

Materials
- No additional materials are needed.

Template
- No template is needed.

Before the Computer
1. Talk about why we celebrate the Fourth of July.
2. Note: Instruct your students to leave the background white for their fireworks pictures. Although fireworks are set off at night, black backgrounds use up a lot of ink!

At the Computer
1. Open *Kid Pix.*
2. Make fireworks pictures by experimenting with the Wacky Paintbrush tool and different Paint Tool options in level one. Change the color you are using for each of the fireworks displays.
3. Choose the stamp tool and add stamps of nighttime objects such as stars and a moon.
4. Print.

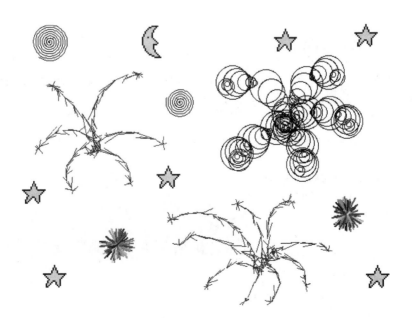

Five Green and Speckled Frogs

Software

- Any drawing software with a frog stamp

Skills Developed

- Counting
- Reading
- Drawing

Materials

- "Five Green and Speckled Frogs" by Robert A. and Marlene J. MacCracken (Peguis Publishers)

Template

- No template is needed.

Before the Computer

1. Sing "Five Green and Speckled Frogs" with the class.
2. Divide students into six small groups.
3. Assign each group a number of frogs (5,4,3,2,1, or 0) to stamp on a log in a pond scene.

At the Computer

1. Open the drawing software.
2. Work with your group to draw a pond scene with a log in it.
3. Stamp your assigned number of frogs on the log.
4. Print.

After the Computer

1. Hang the frog pictures in order from largest to smallest number of frogs.

2. Have students practice reading and singing the song using the pictures as props.

3. You can also put these pictures together in a class-made song book. Allow students to take the book home to share with their families.

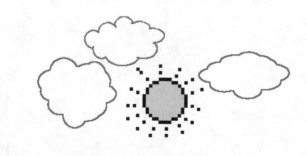

Five Little Monkeys

Software
- Any drawing software, such as Easy Book, that allows you to write a book

Skills Developed
- Rhyming
- Drawing
- Creative writing

Materials
- *Five Little Monkeys Jumping on the Bed* by Eileen Christelow (Houghton Mifflin, 1989)

Template
- No template is needed.

Before the Computer
1. Read aloud *Five Little Monkeys Jumping on the Bed* by Eileen Christelow.
2. Divide the class into small cooperative learning groups. Have each group think of a new version of this story, using different animals and different rhymes.

   Examples: Five little puppies jumping on the couch. One fell off, and he said, "OUCH!"
   Five little ducklings swimming in a pool. One got out when he got too cool.

At the Computer
1. Open the story writing software.
2. Type and illustrate your version of the story.
3. Print.

After the Computer
1. Have the groups stand up and share their stories with the class.
2. Allow the students in each group to take home their version of the story to share with their families. You may wish to send along a copy of the original version with the student-created version. Use a resealable plastic bag for the two books.
3. After all the students have had an opportunity to take the student-made books home, you may wish to donate them to your school library, local public library, or nearby children's hospital.

Five little ducklings swimming in a pool.
One got out when he got too cool.

Flat Stanley

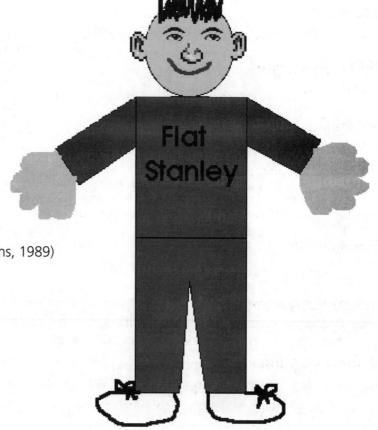

Software
- Any drawing software
- Any word processor

Skills Developed
- Listening
- Drawing
- Reading
- Word processing
- Creative writing

Materials
- *Flat Stanley* by Jeff Brown (HarperCollins, 1989)
- Scissors
- Mailing envelops
- Postage stamps
- Map of the United States
- Star stickers (optional)

Template
- No template is needed.

Before the Computer
- Read aloud *Flat Stanley* by Jeff Brown.

At the Computer
1. Open the drawing software. Use the drawing tools to make a picture of Flat Stanley.
2. Print and cut out Flat Stanley.
3. Open the word-processing software. Type a letter to an out-of-town friend or relative telling about Flat Stanley. Ask the friend or relative to write back to you about Flat Stanley's adventure in his/her home.
4. Print your letter.

After the Computer
1. Place your letter and Flat Stanley inside an envelope.
2. Address the envelope. Be sure to put your return address on it. Place a postage stamp on the envelope, and mail it.
3. When your letter arrives describing Flat Stanley's adventures, share it with the class.

Flowers

Software

- Any drawing software that includes stamps

Skills Developed

- Drawing
- Fine motor

Materials

- Green pipe cleaners
- School photograph of each child
- Clear tape
- Laminating film and laminator or clear contact paper (optional)

Template

- No template is needed.

Before the Computer

- No introductory activities are needed.

At the Computer

1. Open the drawing software.
2. Use any of the drawing tools to make a flower.
3. Choose the stamp tool and stamp a leaf in a separate corner of the page. If your drawing software allows you to change the size of your stamps, make a large-sized leaf. Otherwise, draw your own leaf.
4. Print.

After the Computer

1. Have each student cut out her/his face from a school photograph.
2. Tell students to glue the photographs of their faces in the center of their flowers.
3. Laminate or cover these with clear contact paper.
4. Have students cut out their leaves and flowers and tape them to green pipe cleaners.

Variation

- If you have students' photographs available on disk, you can import them into your drawing software and add them to the centers of the flowers before printing.

Extended Activities

1. These flowers make great Mother's Day gifts.
2. Put together a bouquet with one flower from each child in the class. The bouquet can be given as a special thank-you gift to school personnel such as the principal, secretary, or nurse.

Gingerbread Man

Software
- Any drawing software

Skills Developed
- Fine motor
- Use of drawing tools

Materials
- *The Gingerbread Man* by Karen Schmidt (Scholastic, 1967) or your favorite version

Template
- Gingerbread Man Template

Before the Computer
- Read aloud *The Gingerbread Man* by Karen Schmidt or another version of this story.

At the Computer
1. Open the Gingerbread Man Template.
2. Use any of the drawing tools or stamps to decorate the gingerbread man.
3. Print.

Extended Activities
1. At the beginning of the school year, you may wish to bake a gingerbread man and hide him somewhere in the school. Take students around the school to hunt for the gingerbread man. This is a great way to familiarize students with where the nurse, principal, art room, etc., are located in the school.
2. Type the following sentence on a picture of a gingerbread man: In school you might catch me _____ . Invite students to fill in the blank with something that they like to do at school.

Gorgeous Gifts

Software
- Any drawing software

Skills Developed
- Reading
- Fine motor
- Use of drawing tools

Materials
- No additional materials are needed.

Template
- Gorgeous Gift Template

Before the Computer
- Talk about the kinds of gifts students might like to receive as holiday presents.

At the Computer
1. Open the Gorgeous Gift Template.
2. Decorate the Gorgeous Gift wrapping paper and ribbon using your painting tools.
3. Experiment with painting and drawing tools to make a realistic looking bow on top of the gift.
4. Type your name and the name of a gift you would like to receive to fill in the blanks provided. Example: Anne's gorgeous gift is a new game.
5. Print.

After the Computer
- These pictures can be displayed for the holidays or put into a class book for students to take home to share with their families.

Extended Activity
- It can be fun to prepare a class wish list of all the special gifts your students hope to get. Then this list can be attached to a weekly or monthly parent newsletter.

Happy Holidays

Software
- Any drawing software that includes stamps

Skills Developed
- Fine motor
- Cultural awareness
- Sorting and classification

Materials
- Chart paper
- Markers

Template
- Holiday Chart

Before the Computer
1. Discuss different winter holidays with your class.
2. Have the class work together to create an idea web to show the foods, symbols, and other things that go with each holiday. Draw the idea webs on chart paper.

At the Computer
1. Open the drawing software.
2. Find the Holiday Chart Template on your CD-ROM and import it into your drawing software.
3. Choose the stamp tool and stamp pictures of things that go with each holiday. If you cannot find a stamp of a particular thing, you can draw it using your drawing tools.
4. Print.

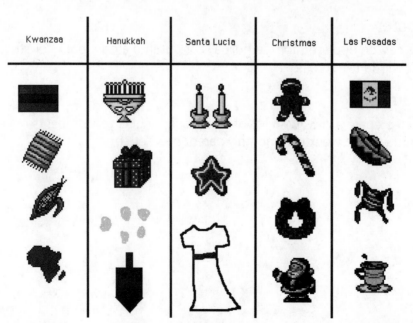

Healthy Meals

Software

- Any drawing software that includes stamps

Skills Developed

- Nutrition

Materials

- No additional materials are needed.

Template

- No template is needed.

Before the Computer

- Talk about the food pyramid and planning a balanced meal.

Lunch

At the Computer

1. Open the drawing software.
2. Decide on one meal (breakfast, lunch, or dinner) that you would like to make. Type the name of your meal at the top of the screen.
3. To make a plate for your food, choose the circle tool and draw a large circle on the center of the screen. If your drawing software does not have a circle tool, use your drawing tools to draw a large circle.
4. Choose stamps to add foods to the plate from each of the five food groups. Use your drawing tools to make pictures of things for which you do not have stamps.
5. To make a place mat, choose a color and a pattern to spill onto the background.
6. Print.

Extended Activities

- Have students draw silverware, a napkin, and a glass to make the place setting look more realistic.

Homes and Addresses

Software

- Any drawing software that allows you to add text

Skills Developed

- Memorization of personal addresses
- Remembering details
- Use of drawing tools

Materials

- No additional materials are needed.

Templates

- Home Template
- Apartment Template

Before the Computer

- For homework, tell students to take a good look at their homes. Have students ask themselves: How many windows does my home have? Is my home built out of bricks, stone, or wood? Are there trees or flowers near my home? Does my home have a garage? Is my home attached to other homes?

At the Computer

1. Open the word-processing software.
2. Depending on where you live, import the Home Template or the Apartment Template from the CD-ROM into your drawing software.
3. Use your drawing tools to decorate the home or apartment. Don't forget to add trees, flowers, and bushes around your home or apartment.
4. Type your address on your home or apartment.
5. Print.

Extended Activity

- Make a large house pattern on a piece of poster board. Allow students to sign the poster board house when they have memorized their home addresses. Display the poster board in the classroom.

How to Make 100

Software

- Any drawing software with stamps

Skills Developed

- Factors of 100
- Multiplication

Materials

- No additional materials are needed.

Template

- No template is needed.

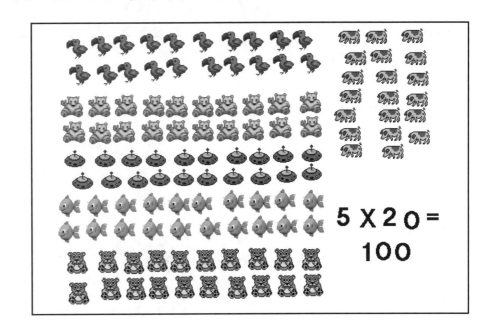

Before the Computer

1. Discuss with the class the different multiplication equations that equal 100 (10 x 10, 2 x 50, 1 x 100, 4 x 25, 5 x 20).
2. Divide the class into five groups and assign an equation to each group.

At the Computer

1. Open the drawing software.
2. Type the assigned equation at the top of the screen.
3. Stamp pictures to illustrate the equation.
4. Print.

After the Computer

- These pictures can be made into a class book of How to Make 100. Students can take the book home to share with their families.

Extended Activity

- This is a wonderful book to make in celebration of the 100th day of school.

Illustrating Poetry

Software

- Any drawing software that allows you to add text

Skills Developed

- Appreciation for poetry
- Interpreting poetry
- Fine motor
- Drawing

Materials

- No additional materials are needed.

Template

- No template is needed.

Before the Computer

- Have each student choose a different poem to illustrate.

At the Computer

1. Open the drawing software.
2. Use the drawing tools to illustrate the poem on the screen.
3. Type the poem somewhere in the picture, too.
4. Print.

After the Computer

- Make a class book of students' favorite poems. Allow students to take the class poetry book home to share with their families.

Extended Activity

- Have the entire class illustrate the same poem. Then invite students to compare and contrast the different illustrations.

In My Closet

Software
- Any drawing software that allows you to add text

Skills Developed
- Drawing
- Fine motor
- Creative writing

Materials
- *There's a Nightmare in My Closet* by Mercer Mayer (Dial, 1968)
- 3.5" x 6" (9.3 cm x 15 cm) rectangles of colored construction paper, one for each student

Template
- No template is needed.

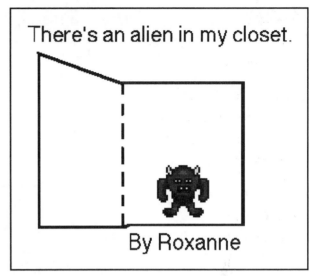

Before the Computer
1. Read aloud *There's a Nightmare in My Closet* by Mercer Mayer.
2. Have students name other things that could be in a closet. List these on chart paper.
3. Have each student sign up to draw one of the things in his/her closet.
4. Give each student a colored construction paper rectangle.

At the Computer
1. Open the drawing software.
2. Draw a picture of the thing that is in your closet. Make sure that you draw the picture smaller than the paper rectangle. To make sure that your picture isn't too big, hold the rectangle vertically (like a door) over your picture on the computer screen. If the picture is larger than the paper rectangle, it is too big. Try drawing a new, smaller picture.
3. Type the following sentence starter somewhere on the screen: There's a(n) _____ in my closet. By _____
4. Fill in the first blank with the name of the thing that is in your closet. Fill in the second blank with your name.
5. Print.

After the Computer
1. Fold a ¼" (0.6 cm) flap along the left side of your construction paper rectangle.
2. Put glue only on the folded flap of the rectangle. Glue the flap to the left of your picture so that your picture can be seen when the "closet door" is opened.
3. Make this into a class book. Encourage students to take the class book home to share with their families. You may wish to send along a copy of the original story by Mercer Mayer with the class book. Use a resealable plastic bag for the two books.

Insect Counting Book

Software
- Any drawing software that includes stamps and allows you to add text

Skills Developed
- Insect recognition
- Counting

Materials
- Chart paper
- Marker
- Stapler or yarn and a hole puncher

Template
- Insect Counting Book 1 Template
- Insect Counting Book 2 Template

Before the Computer
1. As a class, brainstorm a list of different types of insects.
2. Write the names of these insects on chart paper.
3. Display the chart near the computers.

At the Computer
1. Open the drawing software.
2. Find the Insect Counting Book 1 Template on the CD-ROM and import it into your drawing software.
3. Select the stamp tool and find a stamp of an insect. Stamp it one time in the first section.
4. Find a different insect stamp for each section. Place the appropriate number of stamps in each section of the template.
5. Print
6. Repeat the procedure with the Insect Counting Book 2 Template.

After the Computer
1. Cut the pages apart along the lines.
2. Staple the book together or punch two holes and bind the pages together with yarn.

Variation
- You can use stamps to go with a unit or holiday that you are studying. Examples: If you are studying the rainforest, have students make a Rainforest Counting Book. If you are studying Christmas, have students make a Gingerbread Man Counting Book.

Insect Number Cubes Game

Software
- Any drawing software

Skills Developed
- Drawing
- Fine motor
- Counting

Materials
- Blank number cubes, one number cube for each pair of players

Template
- Insect Number Cubes Game Template

Before the Computer
1. Write a 0 or 6 on each side of the number cubes.
2. Assign partners, or allow students to pick partners.

At the Computer
1. Open the drawing software.
2. Find the Insect Number Cubes Game Template on the CD-ROM and import it into your drawing software.
3. Each player should choose a color.
4. Player One should roll the number cube. If you roll a 0, you skip this turn. If you roll a 6, you click on your color and then use your drawing tools to make six legs on one of the insects.
5. Player Two should roll the number cube. If you roll a 0, you skip this turn. If you roll a 6, you click on your color and then use your drawing tools to make six legs on one of the insects.
6. Keep taking turns until all the insects have legs.
7. Count how many insects have legs drawn in each player's color.
8. The winner is the player who has drawn his/her colored legs on the greatest number of insects.

Interesting Insects

Software

- Any drawing software that includes stamps of insects

Skills Developed

- Recognition of insects
- Fine motor

Materials

- No additional materials are needed.

Template

- No template is needed.

Before the Computer

1. Discuss the characteristics of insects, such as that they have three body parts and six legs.
2. You may wish to have students work with partners.

At the Computer

1. Open the drawing software.
2. Find stamps of insects.
3. Select the stamp tool.
4. Stamp all the pictures of insects that you can find.
5. Print.

Note: If you are working with a partner be sure to print two copies.

Extended Activities

- Tell students to type sentences telling why they think insects are interesting.

Invitations

Software
- Any greeting card software that allows you to make custom greeting cards

Skills Developed
- Reading
- Word processing

Materials
- Chart paper
- Marker

Template
- No template is needed.

Before the Computer
1. Decide for which occasion you would like to make invitations. Examples: Open House, School Play.
2. Write all of the important information such as when, where, at what time, and who is invited on chart paper.
3. Display this information near the computers.

At the Computer
1. Open the greeting card software.
2. Type a title on the front of the card.

   Examples: You are invited to _____ .

   Please come to our _____ .

3. Add any appropriate pictures, drawings, or borders to the front of the card.
4. Go to the inside of the card and type all of the important information that is listed on the chart. Add any appropriate pictures, drawings, or borders to the inside of the card.
5. Print.

After the Computer
- Fold the printout into a card.

Extended Activity
- If you have a class e-mail account, you can give parents the option of responding by e-mail. As part of your daily routine, check the class e-mail for messages with your students.

Irresistible Iron-Ons

Software

- Any drawing software

Skills Developed

- Drawing
- Fine motor

Materials

- Heat-transfer paper for your model printer (available at office supply stores)
- White or light-colored T-shirt for each student
- Iron

Template

- No template is needed.

Before the Computer

- Ask each student to bring a white or light-colored T-shirt to school.

At the Computer

1. Open the drawing software.
2. Use the drawing tools, stamps, and graphics to design a picture for your T-shirt. You may wish your design to show something that you are learning about in class. Large graphics that are spread apart on the screen work best for ironing onto shirts. **Note:** Scenes with backgrounds usually come out lighter because they require a lot of heat and a longer ironing time.
3. Print on heat-transfer paper. If you are printing more than one T-shirt, load heat-transfer paper in the printer one sheet at a time.

After the Computer

1. Have students cut around each picture on the heat-transfer paper, leaving a 1/8″ (0.3 cm) border of white around it.
2. Preheat the iron. **Warning:** Never allow students near a hot iron.
3. Carefully read the directions in your heat-transfer paper package.
4. Follow the directions in your heat-transfer paper package to place students' pictures on their T-shirts.

Extended Activity

- At the end of the year, have students make memory shirts. Tell them to use stamps and graphics of things that remind them of special events from the school year. Have them spread these out around the screen. Students can type their grade and the year in their picture. Then allow them to print out their pictures on heat-transfer paper. Use an iron to transfer the pictures onto their T-shirts. Invite students to wear these T-shirts on the last day of school.

Jack-O'-Lanterns

Software

- Any drawing software

Skills Developed

- Drawing
- Creative writing
- Fine motor

Materials

- No additional materials are needed.

Template

- Jack-O'-Lantern Template

At the Computer

1. Open the Jack-O'-Lantern Template.
2. Use the drawing tools and stamps, if they are available, to decorate your jack-o'-lantern.
3. Type or have an adult helper type a sentence describing your jack-o'-lantern.
4. Print.

After the Computer

- The jack-o'-lantern pictures can be mounted and displayed in class, or they can be put into a class book for students to take home to share with their families.

Extended Activity

- You may wish to make a slide show using the jack-o'-lanterns. Record each student reading the sentence that describes his/her jack-o'-lantern.

Jellybean Colors

Software
- *Kid Pix*

Skills Developed
- Use of the Moving Van tool
- Color word recognition
- Fine motor

Materials
- No additional materials are needed.

Template
- Jellybean Colors Template

Before the Computer
- No introductory activities are needed.

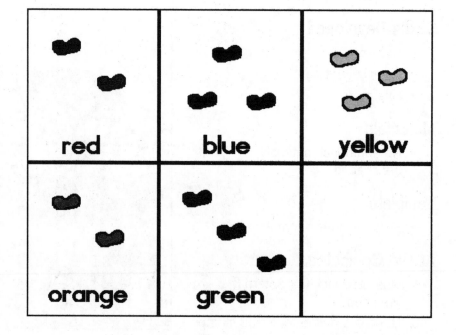

At the Computer
1. Open *Kid Pix*.
2. Find the Jellybean Colors Template on the CD-ROM and import it into *Kid Pix*.
3. Select the Moving Van tool and the square magnet at the bottom of the screen.
4. Place the cursor on the screen and drag it until there is a box around a jellybean.
5. Click on the jellybean in the box and hold down the mouse. Drag the jellybean into the box with the correct color name.
6. Continue dragging jellybeans until you have sorted the colors into the correct boxes.
7. Print or check.

Extended Activity
- As a whole group, build a graph. Have students fill in the cells of a bar graph to show how many of each color.

6					
5					
4					
3					
2					
1					
0	red	orange	yellow	green	blue

Jellybean Counting

Software

- *Kid Pix*

Skills Developed

- Use of the Moving Van tool
- Counting
- Fine motor

Materials

- No additional materials are needed.

Template

- Jellybean Counting Template

Before the Computer

- No introductory activities are needed.

ONE	TWO	THREE
FOUR	FIVE	

At the Computer

1. Open *Kid Pix*.
2. Find the Jellybean Counting Template on the CD-ROM and import it into *Kid Pix*.
3. Select the Moving Van tool and the Square Magnet at the bottom of the screen.
4. Place the cursor where you want it. Then click and drag the cursor across the screen until there is a box around a jellybean.
5. Click on the jellybean in the box and hold down the mouse. Drag the jellybean into one of the sections on the templates.
6. Continue clicking and dragging jellybeans until you have the correct number in each box.
7. Print or check.

Jolly Jokes

Software

- Any drawing software that allows you to add text

Skills Developed

- Writing
- Drawing
- Reading

Materials

- No additional materials are needed.

Template

- No template is needed.

Why did the chicken cross the road?

To get to the other side!

Before the Computer

1. For homework, have students look up and copy their favorite jokes. Remind students that the jokes must be appropriate to share at school.
2. Ask them to bring the jokes to class the following school day.
3. Have students share the jokes in class.

At the Computer

1. Open the drawing software.
2. Type the joke on the screen.
3. Use drawing tools and/or stamps to illustrate the joke.
4. Print.

After the Computer

1. Put the jokes together into a class book. Invite students to take the joke book home to share with their families.
2. After all of the students have had the opportunity to take the joke book home, you may wish to donate it to your school library, local public library, or nearby children's hospital.

Jovial Journal Covers

Software

- Any drawing software that allows you to add text

Skills Developed

- Drawing
- Fine motor

Materials

- Manila file folders, one per student
- Lined notebook paper
- Heavy-duty stapler
- Glue stick

Template

- No template is needed.

Before the Computer

- No introductory activities are needed.

At the Computer

1. Open the drawing software.
2. Make an illustration for the cover of your monthly writing journal. The picture on your journal cover can go with a holiday, season, or a theme that you are studying.
3. Type a title that includes your name on your cover. Example: Peggy's Journal.
4. Print.

After the Computer

1. Use a glue stick to glue your illustration to the file folder.
2. Neatly fill the file folder with notebook paper.
3. With the paper inside the folder, staple along the left-hand side of the file folder using a heavy-duty stapler.

Extended Activities

1. Make new journals for each month or theme.
2. For students who are just beginning to write creative stories, start off the year using journal paper that has only a few lines and blank space to draw. Each month, increase the number of writing lines on each page.

Jumpin' Jewels Game

Software

- *Kid Pix*

Skills Developed

- Number recognition
- Counting
- Addition

Materials

- No additional materials are needed.

Template

- Jumpin' Jewels Template

Before the Computer

- No introductory activities are needed.

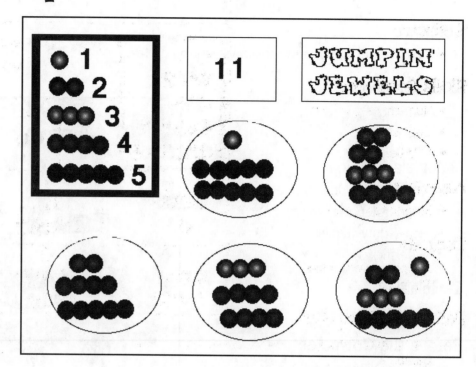

At the Computer

1. Open *Kid Pix.*
2. Find the Jumpin' Jewels Template on the CD-ROM and import it into *Kid Pix.*
3. Type a number between 1 and 12 in the empty box at the top of the screen.
4. Select the Wacky Paintbrush tool. Select the option that looks like colored bubbles with a green background.
5. Fill each circle with the number of jewels that add up to the number you typed in the box. Hold down the OPTION key to make the jewels larger. Use as many jewels as you wish, but change colors to go with the amounts in the key. If you stamp too many of one color, erase them and begin again. Try to fill as many circles as you can with different combinations. Note: The lower the number, the fewer the combinations you will be able to make.
6. Check or print.

Extended Activities

- Each student can play the Jumpin' Jewels Game over and over until they have completed and printed a game board for the numbers 1 through 12. These pages can be printed and stapled into a Jumpin' Jewels Book that students can keep.

Jumpin' Jewels Race

Software
- *Kid Pix*

Skills Developed
- Number recognition
- Counting
- Addition

Materials
- Stopwatch (optional)

Template
- Jumpin' Jewels Race Template

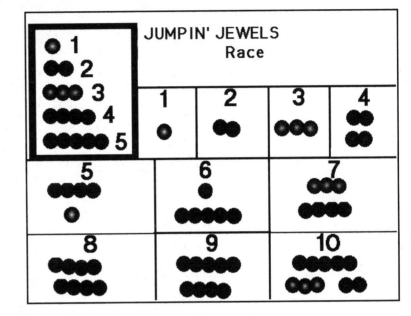

Before the Computer
1. If you have more than one computer available, pick students to race against each other during this game.
2. As an alternative, provide stopwatches for students to time themselves. Then ask them to try to improve their time whenever they play.

At the Computer
1. Open *Kid Pix*.
2. Find the Jumpin' Jewels Template on the CD-ROM and import it into *Kid Pix*.
3. Select the Wacky Paintbrush tool. In level three, select the option that is third from the left. It looks like colored bubbles with a green background.
4. Fill each box with jewels that add up to the number that is in the box. Hold down the OPTION key to make the jewels larger. Use as many jewels as you wish, but change the colors to go with the amounts in the key. If you stamp too many of one color, erase them and begin again. There will be more than one correct answer for each box. However, you only need to show one way to make the number.
5. Check or print.

The Very Hungry Kid

Software
- Any drawing software

Skills Developed
- Drawing
- Reading

Materials
- *The Very Hungry Caterpillar* by Eric Carle (Philomel, 1969)

Template
- No template is needed.

Before the Computer
- Read aloud *The Very Hungry Caterpillar* by Eric Carle.

At the Computer
1. Open the drawing software.
2. Think of something you would like to eat. Draw a picture of or stamp it on the screen.
3. Use your drawing tools to make a picture of your face.
4. Type the following sentence: This hungry kid likes to eat _____ . Complete the sentence by filling in the blank with the name of the food you drew or stamped.

After the Computer
- Make a class book with these pictures. Encourage the children to take the book home to share with their families. In addition, you may wish to send a copy of *The Very Hungry Caterpillar* by Eric Carle. Send both books home in a large resealable bag.

This hungry kid likes to eat radishes.

By Sam

Kings and Queens

Software

- Any drawing software

Skills Developed

- Drawing
- Creative writing
- Fine motor

Materials

- A photograph of each student in PICT format

Template

- No template is needed.

Before the Computer

- No introductory activities are needed.

At the Computer

1. Open the drawing software. Then open the photograph in the drawing software.
2. Using your drawing tools, draw a crown on your head in the photograph.
3. Use the drawing tools and stamps to add jewels and other details to the crown.
4. Type or have an adult helper type the following sentence: If I were the Queen (King), I would _____ . Fill in the blank to tell what you would do if you were queen or king.
5. Print.

After the Computer

1. Display the pictures on a bulletin board, or put them into a class book for students to take home to share with their families.
2. Entitle the bulletin board or the book _____'s Royal Class." Put your name in the blank. Example: Ms. Smith's Royal Class.

Ladybug Math

Software

- Any drawing software

Skills Developed

- Number recognition
- Counting

Materials

- No additional materials are needed.

Templates

- Ladybug Math 1 Template
- Ladybug Math 2 Template (optional)

Before the Computer

- No introductory activities are needed.

8	2	4
5	9	6

At the Computer

1. Open the drawing software.
2. Find the Ladybug Math 1 Template on the CD-ROM and import it into your drawing software.
3. Read the number in each section of the template. Use your drawing tools to make the matching number of dots on the ladybug in each section.
4. In the space provided, type or write how many dots are on each ladybug.
5. Print

Extended Activities

- To practice simple addition facts, open Ladybug Math 2 Template. In this game, students place the dots on each ladybug and then find the sum. Finish the equations by typing the sums, or totals.

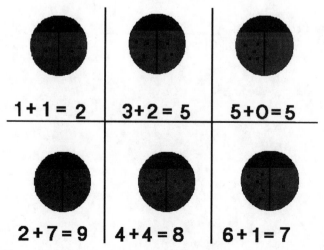

1 + 1 = 2 | 3 + 2 = 5 | 5 + 0 = 5

2 + 7 = 9 | 4 + 4 = 8 | 6 + 1 = 7

Lemonade Signs

Software
- Any drawing software

Skills Developed
- Drawing
- Fine motor
- Reading

Materials
- Chart paper
- Markers

Template
- No template is needed.

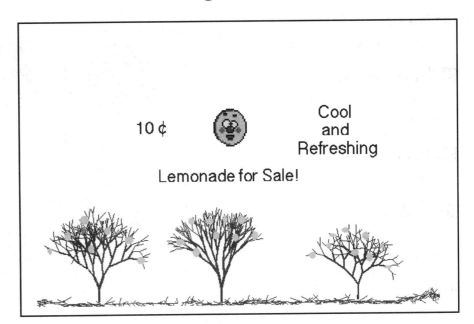

Before the Computer

1. When the weather is hot toward the end of the school year, it is fun to have a lemonade sale.

2. Lemonade can be sold to other students and teachers in the school.

3. Generate a list of words to describe the lemonade. Examples: cold, refreshing, sweet. Write the list on chart paper. Display chart near the computers. Then have the class work together to pick a price to charge for the lemonade. Example: 10 cents per glass.

At the Computer

1. Open the drawing software.
2. Use your stamps and drawing tools to make posters advertising the lemonade sale.
3. Type in some descriptive words on your poster.
4. Print.

Extended Activities

- Your class may wish to use the money they earn from the lemonade sale to buy a special treat like popsicles!

Lollipops

Software

- *Kid Pix* or *Kid Pix Studio*

Skills Developed

- Letter sound recognition

Materials

- Brown construction paper strips
- Glue

Template

- No template is needed.

Before the Computer

- No introductory activities are needed.

At the Computer

1. Open *Kid Pix* or *Kid Pix Studio*.
2. Select the eraser tool.
3. Click on the bomb at the bottom of the page.
4. Click on the screen with your mouse.
5. Select the paint bucket tool and a color. Click on the lollipop where you want that color. You can also click on the black rings to change the color.
6. Print.

After the Computer

1. Cut off any excess white paper from the lollipop.
2. Glue on a brown construction paper strip for the lollipop stick.

Marvelous Mittens

Software
- Any drawing software

Skills Developed
- Drawing
- Symmetry
- Fine motor
- Patterning

Materials
- Mittens
- Scissors
- Yarn
- Clothespins (optional)

Template
- Marvelous Mittens Template

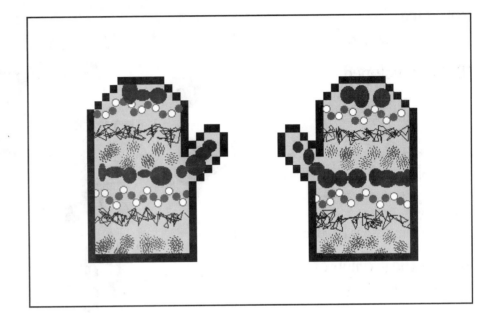

Before the Computer
1. Have students bring in their mittens to sort.
2. Have students compare and contrast the mittens. Look for patterns in the mittens.

At the Computer
1. Open the word-processing software.
2. Find the Marvelous Mitten Template on the CD-ROM and open it in your drawing software.
3. Use the Paint Bucket to fill in both mittens with a background color.
4. Use the drawing tools to make patterns on the mittens with various colors. Remember to make the same patterns and use the same colors on both mittens so you have a matched set when you are finished.
5. Print.

After the Computer
- Have students cut out the mittens.

Extended Activities
- The mittens can be hung on a "clothesline" made of yarn. The line can be strung across a bulletin board or across the classroom. Hang the mittens on the line with clothespins.

Me

Software

- Any drawing software

Skills Developed

- Drawing
- Fine motor

Materials

- Colored construction paper

Template

- No template is needed.

Before the Computer

- No introductory activities are needed.

At the Computer

1. Open the drawing software.
2. Use the drawing tools to make a self portrait.
3. Print the portraits.

After the Computer

- Have students mount their portraits on colored construction paper.

Extended Activities

1. You may wish to have students make portraits at the beginning and end of the school year. This way students can see the improvement in their drawing skills.
2. Portraits can be saved and made into a slide show. This slide show is perfect to show at open house, back-to-school night, or another parent night.

Mix and Match

Software

- Any drawing software that includes stamps

Skills Developed

- Fine motor
- Exploration of stamps

Materials

- 8.5" x 11" (22 cm x 28 cm) colored construction paper

Template

- Mix and Match Template

Before the Computer

- No introductory activities are needed.

At the Computer

1. Open the drawing software.
2. Find the Mix and Match Template on the CD-ROM and import it into your drawing software.
3. Select the stamp tool. Explore the stamps that are available.
4. Choose a person, animal, or monster stamp that is stamped in two separate parts. Example: A head and body stamp and a legs stamp can be used to make a person.
6. Stamp half of the creature in the top section on one side of the template. Stamp the other half in the bottom section on the same side of the template.
7. Follow this same procedure to make the two halves of another creature on the other side of the template.
8. Print.

After the Computer

1. Have students cut apart the pictures along the black lines.
2. Have each student fold a piece of colored construction paper for a book cover.
3. Make a class book so that students can mix and match the different halves of the creatures.

Variation

- Each child can make and print several creatures to make his/her own flip book.

Monster Counting Book

Software

- Any drawing software that allows you to print in different sizes.

Skills Developed

- Drawing
- Counting
- Fine motor

Materials

- 11.5" x 18" (29.3 cm x 46 cm) pieces of construction paper
- Scissors
- Glue

Template

- No template is needed.

Before the Computer

- No introductory activities are needed.

At the Computer

1. Open the drawing software.
2. Use your drawing tools to create a picture of a monster.
3. Print in the smallest or second to smallest size available.

After the Computer

1. Have students cut out their monsters.
2. Make a class counting book using the construction paper. On the first page, write the number 0. On the second page, write the number 1 and glue on one monster. On the third page, write the number 2 and glue on two monsters. Continue in this manner until all of the pages in the book are completed.
3. Make a cover for the book with the title "The Monster Counting Book."
4. Glue any remaining monsters on the front and back covers for decoration.
5. Allow students to take the class book home to share with their families.

Extended Activity

- You can make counting books to go with virtually any theme your class is studying. Suggestions: The Spaceship Counting Book, The Teddy Bear Counting Book, The Zoo Counting Book, and The Tulip Counting Book.

Nifty Names

Software

- *Kid Pix*

Skills Developed

- Practice with Wacky Paintbrush tool
- Penmanship

Materials

- Laminating film and laminator or clear contact paper
- Magnets (optional)
- Glue (optional)

Template

- No template is needed.

Before the Computer

- No introductory activities are needed.

At the Computer

1. Open *Kid Pix.*
2. Select the Wacky Paintbrush tool, a color, and the A option from the first level. Write the first letter of your first name on the screen, starting as far to the left on the screen as possible.
3. Select a different color and paintbrush option for each letter.
4. Print.

After the Computer

- Cut off excess paper.

Extended Activities

1. Students can use their nametags to label their desks, lockers, or cubbies.
2. You may wish to laminate the name tags and glue magnets to the back so they can be easily moved around.

Number Cubes Game

Software
- *Kid Pix*

Skills Developed
- Number recognition
- Counting

Materials
- No additional materials are needed.

Template
- Number Cubes Game Template

Before the Computer
- No introductory activities are needed.

⬚ **3**	⬚ **2**	⬚ **5**
⬚ **5**	⬚ **6**	⬚ **1**

At the Computer
1. Open *Kid Pix*.
2. Find the Number Cubes Game Template on the CD-ROM and import it into *Kid Pix*.
3. Select the Wacky Paintbrush tool and choose the Number Cube from the options on the third level at the bottom of the screen.
4. Click the paintbrush in each of the boxes. Hold down the mouse to "roll" the number cube. Let go of the mouse to stop the number cube.
5. Use the Talking Alphabet Stamps tool to write the number that matches the number of dots on the number cube in each section of the template.
6. Print.

Extended Activity
- To make this game more challenging, have students make two number cubes in each section of the template. Ask them to type an addition equation to go with the two number cubes. Then have them type the sum at the end.

6 + 3 = 9	**4 + 2 = 6**	**3 + 1= 4**
6 + 5 = 11	**1 + 3 = 4**	**2 + 4 = 6**

Number Cubes Magic

Software
- *Kid Pix*

Skills Developed
- Number recognition
- Counting
- Probability basics

Materials
- Two number cubes per student or pair of students

Template
- Number Cubes Magic Template

2	**3**	**4**	**5**	**6**	**7**
8	**9**	**10**	**11**	**12**	

CUBE MAGIC

Before the Computer
1. You may wish to have students pick partners for this activity. Otherwise students can play by themselves.
2. Explain to students that there is no winner in this game. The object is to see which number can be filled with paint first.

At the Computer
1. Open *Kid Pix*.
2. Find the Number Cubes Magic Template on the CD-ROM and import it into *Kid Pix*.
3. Player one rolls two number cubes and adds up the number of dots on both cubes.
4. Choose the Paint Bucket tool and a color. Be sure you do not use black.
5. Spill the paint in the box above the number that is the sum of the dots on the two number cubes. Example: If you roll a 4 and a 3, spill paint in the box above the 7.
6. Player two takes a turn by repeating the directions that player 1 followed in steps 3–5.
7. Players keep taking turns until all of the boxes are filled with paint above one of the numbers.

Extended Activity
- To make this game more exciting, have each player guess which number will reach the top first before they begin playing. Then have players spill paint in the squares of the numbers they are guessing. Be sure they do not use black.

Number Word Match

Software
- Any drawing software

Skills Developed
- Drawing
- Fine motor
- Counting
- Reading number words

Materials
- Scissors
- Large resealable plastic bag
- Laminating film and laminator or clear contact paper (optional)

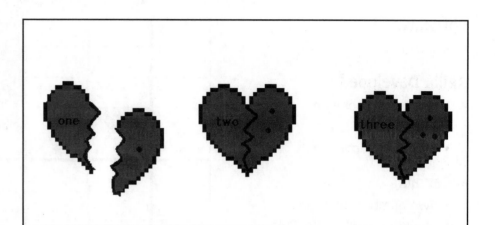

Template
- Number Word Match Template

Before the Computer
1. Write the number words *zero, one, two, three, four, five,* and *six* on chart paper.
2. Post the chart near the computers.

At the Computer
1. Open the drawing software.
2. Find the Number Word Match Template on your CD-ROM and import it into the drawing software.
3. On the first heart, type the word *one* on the left-hand side.
4. Then use your drawing tools to draw one dot on the right-hand side of the heart. Use a rounded pencil point drawing tool if it is available.
5. Continue filling in the other hearts with number words and dots.
6. Print.

After the Computer
1. You may wish to laminate the hearts to improve their durability.
2. Have students cut out the hearts. Then show them how to cut the hearts in half along the zigzag lines.
3. Have students practice matching the dots with the number words.
4. Store the hearts in a resealable plastic bag when students are not using them.

Extended Activity
- For an additional challenge, make a set of hearts for the number words *six, seven, eight, nine, ten, eleven,* and *twelve.* Have students practice matching the dots with these number words.

Number Writing

Software
- Any drawing software

Skills Developed
- Writing numbers
- Fine motor

Materials
- A chart with numbers 0-9 written using correct formation

Template
- No template is needed.

Before the Computer
- Post your number chart near the computers.

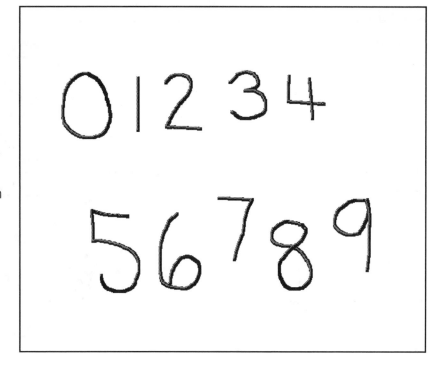

At the Computer
1. Open the drawing software.
2. Use a drawing tool, such as a pencil or paintbrush, to practice writing the numbers 0, 1, 2, 3, 4, 5, 6, 7, 8, and 9 on the screen.
3. Print.

Extended Activities
1. Students can practice writing numbers with the different drawing tools.
2. Have students redo this activity several times during the year. Save their number writing papers. Periodically, allow students to look at their papers so they can see their growth throughout the year.

I'm Nuts About . . .

Software
- Any software that includes drawing tools and stamps

Skills Developed
- Reading
- Creative writing

Materials
- No additional materials are needed.

Template
- I'm Nuts About . . . Template

Before the Computer
- Discuss what it means to be "nuts" about something.

I'm nuts about...

I'm nuts about rainbows, the beach, my friends, rabbits, my teddy bear, candy canes and my pet lizard.

At the Computer
1. Open the drawing software.
2. Find the I'm Nuts About . . . Template on the CD-ROM and import it into the drawing software.
3. Draw or stamp pictures of things that you are nuts about.
4. Type the following sentence: I'm nuts about...
5. Complete the sentence by listing things that you are nuts about. Example: I am nuts about reading, playing football, watching movies, and eating popcorn.
6. Print.

Extended Activities
1. This activity is a great way for students to get to know each other at the beginning of the school year.
2. The pictures can be put into a slide show. Record students telling what they are nuts about to go with their slides. Present the slide show at a special night for parents.

Ocean Pictures

Software

- Any drawing software

Skills Developed

- Drawing
- Fine motor
- Recognition of ocean creatures

Materials

- No additional materials are needed.

Template

- No template is needed.

Before the Computer

- Talk about things you might see in the ocean.

At the Computer

1. Open the drawing software.
2. Use your drawing tools to make a horizontal line to show where the sand meets the water.
3. Choose the Paint Bucket tool to spill tan paint in the sand.
4. Painting the water is optional since it uses a lot of ink.
5. Use stamps of ocean creatures to fill the ocean.
6. Use any of the drawing tools to add details, such as seaweed and bubbles, to the ocean.
7. Print.

Extended Activity

- Before printing, each student can type the following sentence: In the ocean, I can see _____ . Have students fill in the blank with the names of objects and creatures in the ocean. If a student is not able to type, have an adult helper do the typing while the student dictates what he/she sees in the ocean.

Odd and Even

Software

- Any drawing software that includes stamps

Skills Developed

- Counting
- Concept of odd and even

Materials

- No additional materials are needed.

Template

- Odd/Even Template

Before the Computer

- Discuss the difference between odd and even numbers.

At the Computer

1. Open the drawing software.
2. Find the Odd/ Even Template on your CD-ROM and import it into the drawing software.
3. Choose the stamp tool and stamp odd and even amounts in the appropriate sections of the template.
4. Change the stamps for each box.
5. Check for accuracy and print.

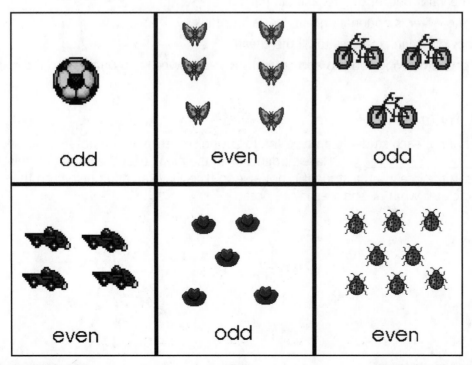

There Was An Old Lady Who Swallowed a Fly

Software

- Any drawing software that includes stamps

Skills Developed

- Listening
- Memorization

Materials

- *There Was an Old Lady Who Swallowed a Fly* by Pam Adams (Playspaces, 1973) or another version of this story

Template

- Old Lady Template

Before the Computer

1. Read aloud any version of *There Was An Old Lady Who Swallowed A Fly.*
2. Encourage the class to try to remember all of the things that the old lady swallows in the story.

At the Computer

1. Open the drawing software.
2. Find the Old Lady Template on the CD-ROM and import it into the drawing software.
3. Try to find stamps of all of the things that the old lady in the story swallowed. Stamp those things in the old lady's stomach. If you cannot find a stamp that you need, you can draw that picture in the old lady's stomach using your drawing tools.
4. You can also use your drawing tools to color the picture of the old lady.
5. Print.

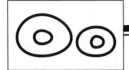

Opposites

Software
- Any drawing software that includes stamps

Skills Developed
- Opposites
- Vocabulary
- Reading

Materials
- No additional materials are needed.

Template
- No template is needed.

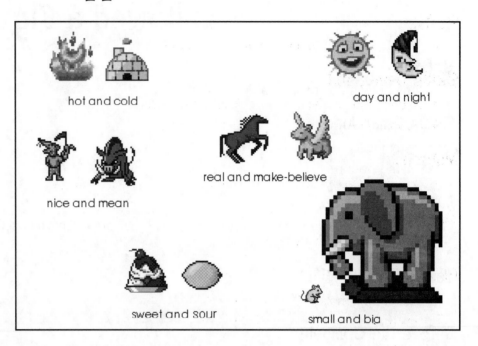

hot and cold

day and night

nice and mean

real and make-believe

sweet and sour

small and big

Before the Computer
1. Suggest some things that are opposites.
2. Then have the class brainstorm a list of other opposites.

At the Computer
1. Open the drawing software.
2. Look for stamps of things that are opposites. Example: An up arrow and a down arrow.
3. Stamp them next to each other on the page.
4. Once the page has several sets of opposites, type the opposite words next to each picture.
5. Print.

After the Computer
1. You can make a class book of opposites.
2. Title each page with a student's name such as "Katie's Opposites."
3. Allow students to take the class book home to share with their families.

Pairs

Software

- Any drawing software that includes stamps

Skills Developed

- Understanding pairs
- Cooperative learning
- Fine motor control
- Use of stamps

Materials

- No additional materials are needed.

Template

- No template is needed.

Before the Computer

1. Talk about things that come in pairs.
2. Divide students into pairs to work on this activity.

At the Computer

1. Open the drawing software.
2. Look through your stamps to find things that come in pairs such as mittens, eyes, and boots.
3. Select the stamp tool and stamp two pictures of each pair found. Be sure to take turns with your partner when you are stamping.
4. Print two copies.

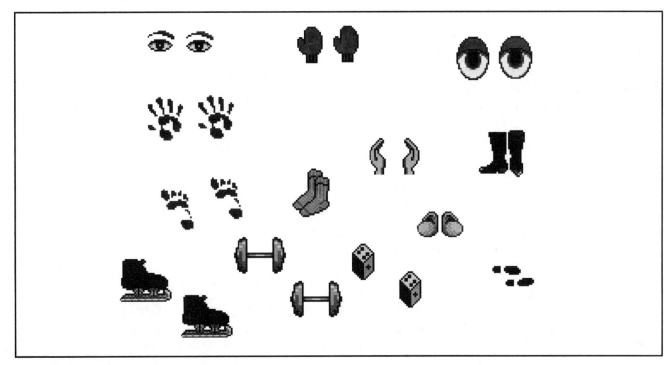

Patchwork Animal Slide Shows

Software
- Any drawing software that includes a Paint Bucket tool
- *Kid Pix Slide Show* (optional)

Skills Developed
- Drawing
- Creative writing
- Fine motor
- Listening

Materials
- *Elmer the Elephant* by David McKee (William Morrow, 1989)
- Chart paper
- Marker

Template
- Patchwork Elephant Template (optional)

Before the Computer
1. Read aloud *Elmer the Elephant* by David McKee.
2. On chart paper, list other animals that could be made of patches.
3. Have each student sign up to draw one of the animals on the list.
4. Designate a folder in which students should save their work.

At the Computer
1. Open the drawing software.
2. **Note:** For younger students, use the Patchwork Elephant Template. Have all the children draw lines for patches on Elmer and practice spilling paint into the different patchwork designs. Otherwise have students choose the pencil tool and a line of medium thickness.
3. Use black to draw the outline of an animal.
4. Draw an eye using the circle tool.
5. Choose the pencil tool and a thin line.
6. Draw a black checkerboard pattern over your animal. Make sure the ends of all your lines touch the outline of the animal so that your paint does not spill from one section to the next.
7. Use the Paint Bucket tool to spill the different colors and patterns onto the patchwork squares.
8. Save your work in the folder designated by your teacher.

Extended Activity
- Make a *Kid Pix Slide Show* using the patchwork animal pictures. Record students telling something about their patchwork animals. Make sure to save the slide show in the same folder as the patchwork pictures. Show your slide show at a special popcorn party or parent night.

Patterns

Software

- Any drawing software that includes stamps

Skills Developed

- Patterning

Materials

- No additional materials are needed.

Template

- No template is needed.

Before the Computer

- No introductory activities are needed.

At the Computer

1. Open the drawing software.
2. Select the stamp tool and choose two or three different stamps.
3. Use the stamps to make a pattern across the top of the page.
4. Type capital letters under the pictures to label your pattern. Example: ABBABB.
5. You may wish to make other rows of patterns on the screen.
6. Print.

Extended Activities

1. The patterns can be made into a class book. For young children who cannot read, you can attach a copy of each child's photograph to her/his pattern so that the students can see which patterns their friends have made.
2. If you have a variety of stamp sets available to you, have students make stamp patterns that fit a specific theme. Examples: Use only rainforest stamps, Thanksgiving stamps, or endangered animal stamps.

Penmanship

Software

- Any drawing software

Skills Developed

- Letter writing
- Fine motor

Materials

- Alphabet chart

Template

- No template is needed.

Before the Computer

- Post an alphabet chart near the computers.

At the Computer

1. Open the drawing software.
2. Use your drawing tools to write the alphabet. Make a pattern on the screen using a capital letter, a lowercase letter, a capital letter, and a lowercase letter. Continue making letters until you have the entire alphabet.
3. If you run out of room, you may need to print what you have done, and finish making the rest of the alphabet on a new screen. Then print the other screen, too.

Extended Activities

1. This can be done with cursive letters, too. For variety, students can practice writing using the different options available with the Wacky Paintbrush tool.
2. You can have students do this activity periodically throughout the year. These writing samples can be saved so students can see their growth.

Perfect Postcards

Software

- Any drawing software that allows you to add text

Skills Developed

- Drawing
- Fine motor

Materials

- Postage stamps
- Photographs of students and class activities saved to disk
- White tagboard

Template

- No template is needed.

Before the Computer

- No introductory activities are needed.

At the Computer

1. Open the drawing software.
2. Import a photograph of a special class activity.
3. Resize your photograph.
4. Draw a white rectangle on the top or bottom of the photograph.
5. In the white rectangle, type a sentence for the front of the postcard.
   Example: Greetings from the Nature Center!
6. Print.

After the Computer

1. Cut out your postcard and glue it onto a piece of white tagboard.
2. On the back of the postcard, draw a vertical line down the center.
3. On one half of the card, write a letter to your parents.
4. Stick the stamp on the upper right-hand corner of the back of the card. Write your parents' address below.
5. Mail the postcard.

Poetry Slide Shows

Software
- Any drawing software and *Kid Pix Slide Show*

Skills Developed
- Drawing
- Poetry appreciation
- Cooperative learning

Materials
- Poems

Template
- No template is needed.

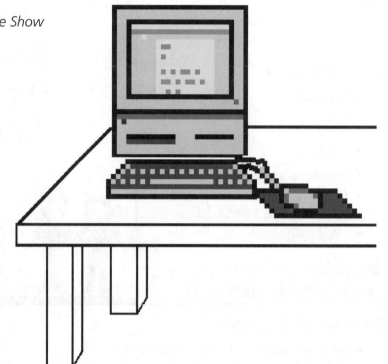

Before the Computer
1. Divide students into small groups.
2. Have each group choose a favorite poem as the theme for a slide show.

At the Computer
1. Open the drawing software.
2. Use your drawing tools to create a title screen for the poem.
3. Make a folder on the desktop, hard drive, or diskette for the title screen. Save the title screen in this folder.
4. Type each line on a new computer screen and create a picture to illustrate it. Save all your pictures in the folder you created.
5. Open *Kid Pix Slide Show*.
6. Import each picture into the slide show, beginning with the title screen.
7. Record the voices of students in your group reading the lines of the poem. Match the lines of the poem with the appropriate pictures in the slide show.
8. Save the slide show in the same folder that the slides are in.

After the Computer
1. Bring in popcorn and play the slide show to the class for fun.
2. Poetry slide shows can be played at parent nights or school assemblies.
3. You may wish to invite your principal to a special preview of the show.

Extended Activity
- If you have access to a digital camera, you may wish to take group pictures to show students who worked together on each of the slide shows. Import the group picture as the last slide in each show.

Polygons

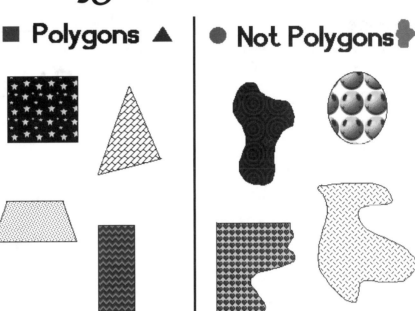

Software
- Any drawing software

Skills Developed
- Recognizing polygons
- Drawing

Materials
- No additional materials are needed.

Template
- Polygon Template

Before the Computer
1. Discuss what a polygon is.
2. Show students pictures of shapes—some that are polygons and some that are not.

At the Computer
1. Open the drawing software.
2. Find the Polygon Template on the CD-ROM and import it into the drawing software.
3. Notice the headings Polygons and Not Polygons on the template. Use the drawing tools to make shapes that go under each heading. Remember that polygons have sides, angles, and vertexes.
4. You can fill in the shapes with any colors or patterns that you like.
5. Print.

Extended Activity
- You can use these shape pictures to play a polygon attribute game. Have a student look at his/her paper and describe a shape for the class. Example: I'm looking at a polygon that has four sides and two of the sides are shorter than the other two. The student who guesses the type of polygon can give the next description.

Pop-Up Facts

Software
- Any drawing software that allows you to add text

Skills Developed
- Research
- Typing
- Remembering facts

Materials
- 8.5" x 11" (22 cm x 28 cm) piece of tagboard for each student (optional)

Template
- No template is needed.

Before the Computer
- No introductory activities are needed.

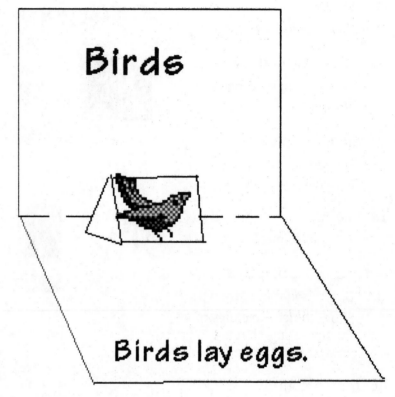

At the Computer
1. Open the drawing software.
2. Type the name of the animal or subject at the top of the page.
3. Type one or more facts that you know about that animal or subject.
4. In the center of the screen, stamp or draw a picture to illustrate your fact(s).
5. Print.

After the Computer
1. Fold your paper in half horizontally so that the picture is on the outside.
2. Cut a small, vertical slit on each side of the picture.
3. Unfold your paper and fold it back again along the same fold so that the picture is on the inside. Then pop out your picture.
4. You may wish to glue an 8.5" x 11" (22 cm x 28 cm) piece of tagboard that is folded in half horizontally so that your picture will stand up on a desk or counter for display.

Precise Punctuation

Software
- Any word processor

Skills Developed
- Punctuation
- Reading
- Creative writing

Materials
- An overhead projector and transparencies made for use with your printer. These are available at office supply stores and from mail order computer catalogs.

Template
- No template is needed.

? Do you like cats !
I like to ride the bus
! School is great ?

Before the Computer
- Specify a large size font and a font style for all students to use for this project.

At the Computer
1. Open the word-processing software.
2. Type three sentences, each one ending in a different punctuation mark (., !, ?). However, do not type the punctuation marks.
3. Print on transparency paper that is made for your printer.
4. On a new screen, type some periods, question marks, and exclamation points in a large font so that each is ¼–1" (0.6–2.5 cm) tall. Use the tab key to space them apart.
5. Print the punctuation marks on transparency paper.
6. Cut out each punctuation mark within a 1" (2.5 cm) square.

Extended Activity
- Take turns showing different students' sentences on the overhead projector. Have volunteers come up to the projector to place the proper punctuation square at the end of each sentence. Then have the rest of the class check the punctuation for accuracy.

Pretty Pins

Software
- Any software with stamps

Skills Developed
- Drawing
- Fine Motor

Materials
- Laminating film and laminator or clear contact paper
- Glue gun (for adult use only)
- Craft pin back
- Sequins
- Rhinestones
- Small beads (optional)

Template
- No template is needed.

Before the Computer
- No introductory activities are needed.

At the Computer
1. Open the drawing software.
2. Draw or stamp a picture that is 1–3" (2.5–8 cm) tall and wide.
3. Print.

After the Computer
1. Have students cut out the picture leaving a ⅛" (0.3 cm) border of white around it.
2. Laminate the picture or cover it with clear contact paper.
3. Use a hot glue gun to put a pin on the back of each picture. **Warning:** Never allow students to use a hot glue gun.
4. These pins make great gifts for holidays, Mother's Day, parent helpers, or teachers.

Extended Activities
- Ask adult volunteers to use hot glue guns to add sequins, rhinestones, and small beads to the pins.

Puzzles

Software
- Any drawing software

Skills Developed
- Drawing
- Fine motor control
- Exploration of drawing tools

Materials
- Large resealable plastic bags
- Laminating film and laminator or clear contact paper

Template
- No template is needed.

Before the Computer
- No introductory activities are needed.

At the Computer
1. Open the drawing software.
2. Draw and color a picture using your drawing tools and stamps. If ready-made pictures are available for coloring you can choose one of these to color instead.
3. Print two copies of your picture.

After the Computer
1. Laminate the pictures or cover them with clear contact paper.
2. Have students staple the first copy to a large resealable plastic bag.
3. Tell students to cut the second copy apart into puzzle pieces. Have them put their puzzle pieces in their plastic bags.
4. These make great gifts for brothers, sisters, or friends. Your students might also like to donate their puzzles to a nearby children's hospital or other children's charity.

Extended Activity
- Make original puzzles related to a particular unit or theme your class is studying. Store them in plastic resealable bags as described above. Invite students to put the puzzles together.

Quilts

Software
- Any drawing software

Skills Developed
- Knowledge of holidays and seasons

Materials
- Colored construction paper
- Tape
- Bows and buttons for decoration (optional)
- Pinking shears (optional)
- Hot glue gun (optional)

Template
- No template is needed.

Before the Computer
1. Choose two colors that go along with your theme.
2. Cut 9" x 11" (23 cm x 28 cm) pieces of construction paper in those colors.
3. Tape the construction paper together to make a quilt. Alternate the colors to make a pattern.
4. The size of your quilt will depend on the number of pictures your class will make.
5. Turn the quilt over so that the tape is on the back.

At the Computer
1. Open the drawing software.
2. Use your drawing tools to make a picture that goes with the season, holiday, or theme that you are studying.
3. Print.

After the Computer
1. Cut any excess white paper off of the picture. For an added design, you may wish to cut the excess paper off with pinking shears.
2. Glue your quilt square somewhere on the class quilt.
3. After the glue has dried, display the class quilt.

Extended Activities
- For decoration, add buttons and/or bows on the corners where the pieces of construction paper meet. A hot glue gun is the best way to securely fasten these items.

Race from 100

Software

- *Kid Pix*

Skills Developed

- Subtraction

Materials

- No additional materials are needed.

Template

- Race from 100 Template

Before the Computer

- No introductory activities are needed.

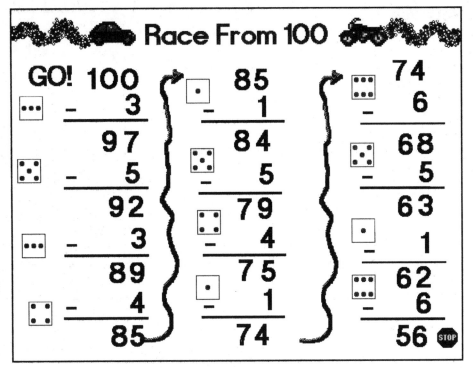

At the Computer

1. Open *Kid Pix*.
2. Find the Race from 100 Template on the CD-ROM and import it into *Kid Pix*.
3. Choose the Wacky Paintbrush tool and the Number Cube option.
4. Stamp one number cube next to each blank equation as shown in the example below.
5. Select the Talking Alphabet Stamps tool.
6. Start with 100 and subtract each amount shown on the number cubes.
7. Type the numbers for each equation.

Extended Activities

- Have pairs of students compete against each other. Keep track of the last answer given by each student. The student who ends with the smallest number after 12 rolls of the number cube is the winner.

Radical Riddles

Software
- Any software that allows you to custom make greeting cards

Skills Developed
- Reading
- Word processing

Materials
- Assorted riddle books

  Suggestions:

  Riddle City, USA: A Book of Geography Riddles by Marco and Giulio Maestro (HarperCollins, 1994)

  Riddle-icious by J. Patrick Lewis (Dial, 1995)

  Riddle Rhymes by Charles Ghigna (Hyperion, 1995)

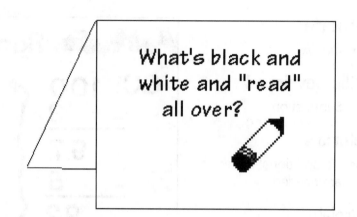

Template
- No template is needed.

Before the Computer
- Provide time for students to read riddle books and choose their favorite riddles.

At the Computer
1. Open the greeting card software.
2. Type the riddle on the cover of the card. Add any pictures, drawings, or borders to the front of the card that relate to your riddle.
3. Go to the inside of the card and type the answer to the riddle. You can also add any appropriate pictures, drawings, or borders to the inside of the card.
4. Print.

After the Computer
- Fold the printout into a card.

Extended Activities
1. You can make a 3-dimensional display of students' riddles on a bulletin board or wall. Title the display "Radical Riddles."
2. Mount the riddles on 8.5" x 11" (22 cm x 28 cm) pieces of construction paper and make a class pop-up riddle book. Encourage students to take the riddle book home to share with their families.

Rebus Story

Software

- Any drawing software that includes stamps and allows you to add text.

Skills Developed

- Creative writing
- Reading

Materials

- No additional materials are needed.

Template

- No template is needed.

Before the Computer

- Tell students that they will need to pick a few stamps that they will use to create a story.

At the Computer

1. Open the drawing software. Choose a few stamps for your story.
2. Type a creative story. Use the stamps you have chosen instead of words whenever possible.
3. Print.

After the Computer

- Share your story with the class.

Variation

- For younger students, the teacher may want to make rebus stories based on classic books such as *The Three Bears*. Print the rebus story and make multiple copies for your class to read.

> Once upon a time there was a 🐭.
> It lived in a little 🏠. One day, the 🐭 decided to pick some 🌼🌼🌼🌼. Then the 🐭 lived happily ever after.

Rhyming

Software
- Any drawing software with stamps

Skills Developed
- Rhyming

Materials
- No additional materials are needed.

Template
- No template is needed.

Before the Computer
- No introductory activities are needed.

dog   frog

At the Computer
1. Open the drawing software.
2. Select two stamps with picture names that rhyme and stamp them on the screen.
3. Type the name of each picture underneath.
4. Print. If your software gives you the option to print using a small size, you may choose to do this.

After the Computer
1. Cut off excess white paper.
2. Put the pages with rhyming pairs together to make a class book.

Extended Activities
1. This can be made into a class mini-book.
2. You may wish to reproduce all of the children's pages to make a mini-rhyming book for each child to keep.

Seasonal Hat

Software
- Any drawing software with stamps

Skills Developed
- Four seasons
- Fine motor

Materials
- 4.5" x 11" (11.3 cm x 28 cm) strip of construction paper for each student
- Stapler

Template
- Seasons Template

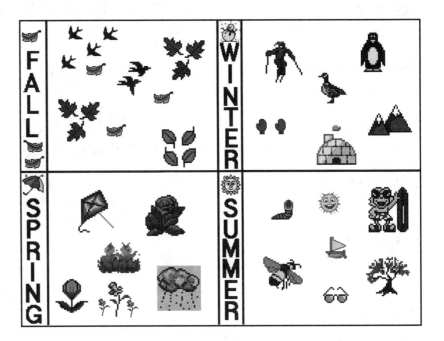

Before the Computer
- No introductory activities are needed.

At the Computer
1. Open the drawing software.
2. Find the Seasons Template on the CD-ROM and import it into your drawing software.
3. Find stamps of things that can be seen in any of the four seasons.
4. Stamp appropriate stamps in each section of the template.
5. Print.

After the Computer
1. Cut off excess paper.
2. Cut in half along the horizontal black line.
3. Staple the spring section to the end of the winter section. Then staple all four seasons onto a strip of construction paper.
4. Help students place the band around their heads and staple the ends together.

Secret Message

Software
- *Kid Pix*

Skills Developed
- Creative writing
- Fine motor
- Drawing

Materials
- No additional materials are needed.

Template
- No template is needed.

Before the Computer
- No introductory activities are needed.

At the Computer
1. Open *Kid Pix*.
2. Select the Wacky Paintbrush tool and choose the Alphabet Line option (ABC).
3. Go to Toolbox on the menu bar. Click and drag down to the Talking Alphabet tool.
4. Type your secret message in the box and click OK. Make sure the message is only a few sentences long. Examples: I like you! or Have a nice day!
5. Drag your mouse across the top of the screen and down the right-hand side to see the message. When you get to the bottom of the screen, stop and begin dragging the message a second time down the left-hand side of the screen and across the bottom.

   Note: If you drag the message from right to left, the words will be backwards. If you drag the message from the bottom of the screen to the top of the screen, the message will be upside down.

6. Add stamps or draw pictures to go with your secret message.
7. Print.

After the Computer
- Deliver your secret message.

Extended Activities
- Have students participate in a Secret Pals activity. Place every student's name on a strip of paper and place the names in a container. Have students draw names out of the container. Ask them not to tell whose name they have picked. Have students write and deliver secret messages to their Secret Pal over the period of one week. At the end of the week, allow students to try to guess who their Secret Pals were.

Shape Book

Software

- Any drawing software that includes stamps

Skills Developed

- Shape recognition

Materials

- No additional materials are needed.

Templates

- Circle Template
- Rectangle Template
- Square Template
- Triangle Template

Before the Computer

- No introductory activities are needed.

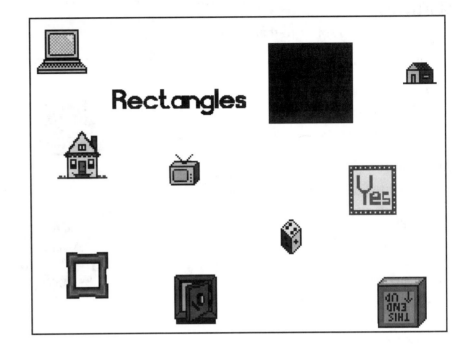

At the Computer

1. Open the drawing software.
2. Find one of the shape templates on your CD-ROM and import it into the drawing software.
3. Choose the stamp tool.
4. Find stamps of include that particular shape and stamp them on the template.
5. Print.

After the Computer

- You can put all of the shape papers together into a class book, or each student can make a picture for each shape and make his/her own book.

Shape-O-Rama

Software

- Any drawing software that allows you to add text

Skills Developed

- Shape recognition
- Reading shape words
- Drawing shapes

Materials

- No additional materials are needed.

Template

- No template is needed.

Before the Computer

- No introductory activities are needed.

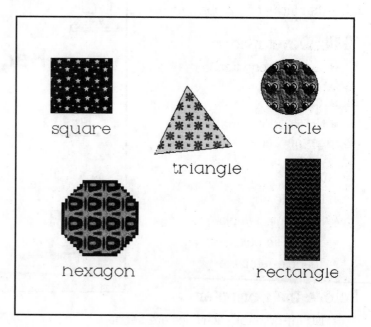

At the Computer

1. Open the drawing software.
2. Use the drawing tools to make shapes.
3. Fill in the shapes with any colors or patterns that you like.
4. Next to each shape type its name.
5. Print.

Extended Activities

- You can use these shape pictures to play a shape attribute game. Have a student look at his/her paper and describe a shape for the class. Example: I'm looking at a shape that has four sides and two of the sides are shorter than the other two. The student who guesses the shape can give the next description.

Shape Land

Software

- Any drawing software that allows you to draw shapes

Skills Developed

- Shape recognition
- Drawing
- Fine motor

Materials

- No additional materials are needed.

Template

- No template is needed.

Before the Computer

1. Have students look for shapes around the classroom.
2. Discuss how there are many shapes in the real world.

At the Computer

1. Open the drawing software.
2. Use your drawing tools to create a scene made up of different shapes.
3. Add colors and details to your picture.
4. Make a shape key in one of the corners of your picture.
5. For your key, draw a small copy of each of the shapes you used in the picture.
6. Count how many of each shape you used in your picture and type that number next to each shape in your key.
7. Print.

Extended Activity

- You can compare pictures to see which student used the most circles, squares, rectangles, and triangles.

Spider Art

Software
- Any drawing software

Skills Developed
- Drawing
- Fine motor
- Exploration of drawing tools

Materials
- No additional materials are needed.

Template
- No template is needed.

Before the Computer
- Talk about the characteristics of spiders.
  Examples: They have 2 body parts, 2–8 eyes, and 8 legs.

At the Computer
1. Open the drawing software.
2. Use your drawing tools to draw a spider's body and head. If you have a circle tool, you can use it to make the spider's body and head.
3. Use your drawing tools to draw eight legs on your spider.
4. Add any other details to make your spider look realistic. You can also draw scenery around the spider.
5. Print.

Extended Activity
- For an added math twist, have students write number sentences to describe the number of legs on the spider.

Spider Number Cubes Game

Software
- Any drawing software

Skills Developed
- Drawing
- Fine motor
- Counting

Materials
- Blank number cubes, one cube for every pair of players

Template
- Spider Number Cubes Game Template

Before the Computer
1. Write 0 or 8 on each of side of the number cubes.
2. Assign partners, or allow students to pick their own partners.

At the Computer
1. Open the Spider Number Cubes Game Template in your drawing software.
2. Have each player choose a color.
3. Player One rolls the number cube. If you roll 0, you skip this turn. If you roll 8, you use your chosen color and a drawing tool to make eight legs on one of the spiders.
4. Player Two rolls the number cube. If you roll 0, you skip this turn. If you roll 8, you use your chosen color and a drawing tool to make eight legs on one of the spiders.
5. Keep taking turns until all the spiders have legs.
6. Then count how many spiders have legs drawn in each player's color.
7. The winner is the player who has drawn his/her colored legs on the greatest number of spiders.

Spooky Stories

Software

- Any drawing software
- Any word processor

Skills Developed

- Drawing
- Fine motor
- Creative writing
- Word processing

Materials

- No additional materials are needed.

Template

- No template is needed.

Before the Computer

- No introductory activities are needed.

At the Computer

1. Open the drawing software.
2. Use your drawing tools to make a horizontal line for the horizon.
3. Then draw and stamp Halloween pictures to make a spooky scene.
4. Print.
5. Open the word-processing software.
6. Type a creative story about your Halloween picture.
7. Print.

After the Computer

1. Pictures and stories can be mounted on construction paper to be displayed.
2. If you prefer, put the pictures and stories together into a class book. Allow students to take the class book home to share with their families.

Stamp a Rainbow

Software
- Any drawing software with stamps available

Skills Developed
- Exploration of stamps
- Drawing
- Fine motor

Materials
- No additional materials are needed.

Template
- No template is needed.

Before the Computer
- No introductory activities are needed.

At the Computer
1. Open the drawing software.
2. Look for stamps that are the color red.
3. Stamp all of the red stamps you can find in an arch.
4. Look for stamps that are orange.
5. Stamp all of the orange stamps you can find in an arch above the red arch.
6. Continue stamping arches in the order of the colors of the rainbow (red, orange, yellow, green, blue, purple).
7. Use your drawing tools to add details such as clouds.
8. Print.

After the Computer
- Display the stamp rainbows up in the clouds. Do this by making your own cloud border for a bulletin board. Cut light blue strips of construction paper that are 2" (5 cm) wide. Take cotton balls and pull them apart. Glue clumps of cotton along the light blue strips so that they look like clouds. Your students will enjoy helping you make these original borders.

Star Students

Software

- Any drawing software that allows you to add text

Skills Developed

- Vocabulary
- Self-confidence

Materials

- Photograph of each child (optional)

Template

- Star Student Template.

Before the Computer

- Pick a Star Student.

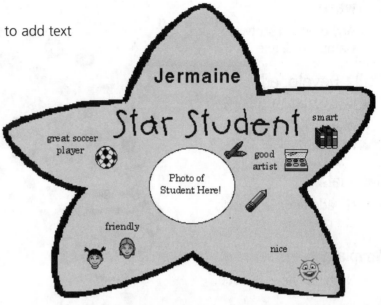

At the Computer

1. Open the drawing software.
2. Find the Star Student Template and import it into the drawing software.
3. Type the Star Student's name on the star.
4. If a photograph of the Star Student is available, import it into the center of the star.
5. Leave the template on the screen for a period of time to allow several students to add positive words or phrases about the Star Student.
6. Have students add appropriate pictures or stamps to go with their words or phrases.
7. Print.

After the Computer

1. Share all of the positive comments with the class.
2. Hang the stars in a special place in the classroom.
3. These stars can be a special touch to any student's portfolio.

Stars

Software

- Any drawing software that has a five-pointed star stamp

Skills Developed

- Counting by fives
- Fine motor

Materials

- No additional materials are needed.

Template

- Stars Template

Before the Computer

- No introductory activities are needed.

At the Computer

1. Open the drawing software.
2. Find the Stars Template on your CD-ROM and import it into the drawing software.
3. Find the star stamp.
4. Stamp one star in the top row labeled five and say, "Five."
5. Stamp two stars in the next row down labeled ten and say, "Five, ten."
6. Continue stamping the correct number of stamps in each row until all rows are complete.
7. Print or check.

Ten Apples Up On Top

Software

- Any drawing software that has an apple stamp

Skills Developed

- Drawing
- Fine motor
- Counting
- Listening

Materials

- *Ten Apples Up On Top!* by Theo LeSeig (Random, 1961)

Template

- Ten Apples Up On Top! Template

Before the Computer

1. Read aloud *Ten Apples Up On Top!* by Theo LeSeig.
2. Practice counting the apples in the book as you read.

At the Computer

1. Open the drawing software.
2. Find the Ten Apples Up On Top! Template on your CD-ROM and import it into the drawing software.
3. Select the apple stamp.
4. Stamp ten apples on each of the animals' heads. For variety, you can edit the stamp or use the Paint Bucket tool to spill green and yellow paint onto the apples.
5. Check for accuracy and print.

Extended Activity

- For an added challenge, you can make a color pattern using the apples on top of each of the animals' heads. Example: red, yellow, green, red, yellow, green, etc.

Book of Ten

Software

- Any drawing software with stamps that allows you to add text

Skills Developed

- Simple addition facts
- Counting

Materials

- No additional materials are needed.

Template

- No template is needed.

Before the Computer

- No introductory activities are needed.

At the Computer

1. Open the drawing software.
2. Choose two stamps to use.
3. Stamp less than ten pictures (1–9) of the first stamp chosen.
4. Stamp the second stamp enough times so that you have a total of ten pictures on the screen.
5. Type an addition equation to go with the stamps.
6. Print.

After the Computer

1. These equations can be put together to make a class Book of Ten.
2. Students can take this book home to share with their families.

Extended Activities

1. Have students can make their own Mini-Books of Ten. Each student can print his/her picture in a small size if this option is available with your drawing software. Then make more pages for the book by having each page show a different combination of addends that equal ten.
2. Make a Book of Five, a Book of Twenty, etc.

Terrific Trees

Software
- *Kid Pix* or *Kid Pix Studio*

Skills Developed
- Practice using the Wacky Paintbrush tool
- Environmental awareness

Materials
- No additional materials are needed.

Template
- No template is needed.

Before the Computer
- Discuss the importance of trees to people and the environment.

At the Computer
1. Open *Kid Pix* or *Kid Pix Studio*.
2. Use your drawing tools to experiment with drawing trees.
3. Select the Wacky Paintbrush and find the Fractal Trees option.
2. Click and drag the mouse across the screen to make a tree.
4. Using the Wacky Paintbrush tool, again, find the Pine Tree option. Click and drag the mouse across the screen to make this tree.
5. Optional: Type a slogan such as "SAVE THE TREES" on the screen.
6. Print.

Extended Activity
- These pictures can be hung around the school for Earth Day!

124

Under My Bed

Software

- Any drawing software that allows you to add text

Skills Developed

- Drawing
- Fine motor
- Creative writing

Materials

- *There's an Alligator Under My Bed* by Mercer Mayer (Dial, 1987) or *There's a Monster Under My Bed* by James Howe (Atheneum, 1986)
- 3.5" x 6" (9.3 cm x 15 cm) rectangles of colored construction paper
- Glue

There's a frog under my bed.

Template

- No template is needed.

Before the Computer

1. Read aloud *There's an Alligator Under My Bed* by Mercer Mayer or *There's a Monster Under My Bed* by James Howe.
2. On chart paper, list other things that could be found under a bed.
3. Have each student sign up to draw one of the things under his/her bed.
4. Give each student a colored construction paper rectangle.

At the Computer

1. Open the drawing software.
2. Draw a picture of the thing that is under your bed. Make sure that you draw it smaller than the paper rectangle. To make sure that your picture isn't too big, hold the rectangle horizontally (like a bed) over your picture on the computer screen. If the picture is larger than the paper rectangle, it is too big. Try drawing a new, smaller picture.
3. Type the following sentence starter somewhere on the screen: There's a(n) _____ under my bed. By _____
4. Fill in the first blank with the name of the thing that is under your bed. Fill in the second blank with your name.
5. Print.

After the Computer

1. Fold a ¼" (0.6 cm) flap along the top of your construction paper rectangle.
2. Put glue only on the folded flap of the rectangle. Glue the flap to the left of your picture so that your picture can be seen under the bed when the "blanket" is lifted.
3. Make this into a class book. Encourage students to take the class book home to share with their families. You may wish to send along a copy of the original story by Mercer Mayer with the class book. Use a resealable plastic bag for the two books.

Vacation

Software

- Any drawing software with stamps

Skills Developed

- Sorting
- Classifying
- Exploration of stamps

Materials

- Chart paper
- Marker
- File folder (optional)
- Tagboard (optional)
- Stapler (optional)

Template

- Vacation Suitcase Template

Before the Computer

1. Talk about things that you might need to bring on a vacation and list these on chart paper.
2. Talk about things that you would not bring in a suitcase. Examples: fruit, a bird.

At the Computer

1. Open the drawing software.
2. Find the Vacation Suitcase Template on the CD-ROM and import it into the drawing software.
3. Stamp all of the things that you might need on a vacation in the suitcase.
4. Print.

Extended Activity

- Glue your suitcase picture inside a manila file folder. Trace two copies of a suitcase handle pattern on tagboard. Cut out the suitcase handles. Turn the file folder so that the fold is on the bottom. Center the handles on the top of the folder, and staple one to each side. You may wish to type out a luggage tag to attach to your suitcase.

Visits

Software

- Any drawing software that allows you to add text

Skills Developed

- Drawing
- Fine motor
- Creative writing

Materials

- No additional materials are needed.

Template

- No template is needed.

Before the Computer

- Discuss places that would be fun to visit.

At the Computer

1. Open the drawing software.
2. Use the drawing tools and stamps to create a picture of a place that you would like to visit.
3. Type a few sentences about the place you would like to visit. Explain why you would like to visit that place.
4. Print.

Extended Activities

1. You can make a fun display in the classroom of the places your students would like to visit.
2. These pictures and stories also make an interesting slide show. Just save all the pictures in a special slide show folder. You can record your students' voices telling about the places they would like to visit.

Vowel Mobiles

Software
- Any drawing software with stamps

Skills Developed
- Recognizing vowels
- Short vowel sounds
- Exploration of stamps

Materials
- Wire hanger
- Glue
- Scissors

Templates
- Vowel A, E, I, Template
- Vowel O, U, Template

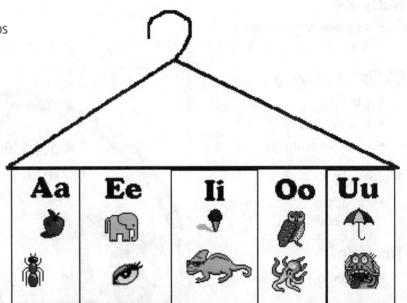

Before the Computer
1. Discuss the sounds that each short vowel represents.
2. Suggest some words that start with each short vowel.

At the Computer
1. Open the drawing software.
2. Find Vowel A, E, I Template and Vowel O,U Template on the CD-ROM and import them into your drawing software.
3. Stamp the things that begin with each vowel sound in the appropriate section on the templates. For the letter Uu, you can stamp things that are "ugly" or arrows that go "up" since there are not many stamps available. You can also use your drawing tools to draw pictures of things that begin with each vowel sound in the appropriate sections.
4. Print.

After the Computer
1. Cut off excess white paper.
2. Cut along vertical solid lines.
3. Fold each top part back along the dotted line
4. Glue each strip of paper over the horizontal part of the hanger.

Extended Activity
- Open Vowel Template 2 and repeat the above instructions.

128

There's a Dragon in my Wagon

Software

- Any drawing software that allows you to add text

Skills Developed

- Listening
- Drawing
- Creative writing
- Reading

Materials

- *There's a Dragon in My Wagon* by JoAnne Nelson

Template

- Wagon Template

Before the Computer

1. Read aloud *There's a Dragon in My Wagon* by JoAnne Nelson.
2. As a class, list other fun and silly things that you could carry in a wagon.
3. List students' suggestions on chart paper.
4. Have each student sign up for one of the things on the list to draw on the computer.

At the Computer

1. Open the drawing software.
2. Find the Wagon Template on the CD-ROM and import it into the drawing software.
3. Use your drawing tools to draw your assigned item in the wagon.
4. Type the following sentence: There's a(n) _____ in my wagon.
5. Fill in the blanks with the name of the picture that you drew in your wagon. Then add your name below the picture.
6. Print.

After the Computer

1. Make a class book with all the pictures.
2. Place a copy of the class book and *There's a Dragon in My Wagon* by JoAnne Nelson in a resealable plastic bag.
3. Encourage students to take the books home to share with their families.

Wanted Posters

Software
- Any drawing software

Skills Developed
- Drawing
- Fine motor
- Creative writing

Materials
- Photograph of each child on disk

Template
- No template is needed.

Before the Computer
- Have students think of positive things about themselves.

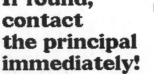

Wanted!

If found, contact the principal immediately!

Last seen at school.

Joe Smith
For being a great artist

At the Computer
1. Open the drawing software.
2. Import your photograph into the drawing software.
3. Decorate the wanted poster by adding a ready-made frame or drawing your own frame.
4. Add text such as the following: WANTED—For being a good reader, helping my friends, and doing my homework on time.
5. Print.

After the Computer
- Ask permission to display the poster around the school.

Watermelon Math

Software

- Any drawing software

Skills Developed

- Drawing
- Counting
- Addition
- Subtraction
- Fine motor

Materials

- No additional materials are needed.

Template

- Watermelon Template

$$4 + 3 = 7$$

Before the Computer

- No introductory activities are needed.

At the Computer

1. Open the drawing software.
2. Find the Watermelon Template on the CD-ROM and import it into the drawing software.
3. Draw some seeds in the watermelon. Use white for some of the seeds and black for the other seeds.
4. Type an addition or subtraction equation to go with the two different colored seeds.
5. Print.

After the Computer

1. Watermelon Math equations can be displayed on a picnic-theme bulletin board.
2. Simply cover the bulletin board with a checkered tablecloth or wrapping paper.
3. Then staple the watermelon pictures on top.

Web About Me

Software
- Any drawing software

Skills Developed
- Reading
- Vocabulary
- Building self-concept
- Use of idea web

Materials
- A photo of each child on disk (optional)

Template
- Web About Me

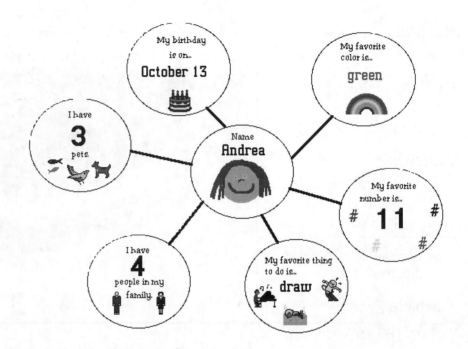

Before the Computer
- For homework, have students find out and write down special information about themselves.

At the Computer
1. Open the drawing software.
2. Find the Web About Me Template and import it into the drawing software.
3. Fill in information about yourself on the web.
4. Copy and paste the your photo from the disk onto the center circle of the web. If a photograph is not available, draw your face where the photo would go.
5. Print.

After the Computer
- Webs can be displayed or put together into a class book for students to take home to share with their families.

Extended Activity
- Students can make original webs using any drawing software or by using a webbing software.

Variation
- If you do not have student photos on disk, have students glue their photos in the center of their webs after printing them.

Web Buddies

Software

- Any Internet connection

Skills Developed

- Use of the Internet
- Cooperative learning

Materials

- Favorite Web site address
- Copies of an Internet Scavenger Hunt prepared ahead of time by the teacher
- Pencils

Template

- No template is needed.

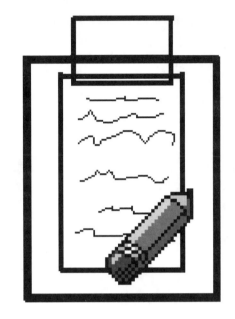

Before the Computer

1. Develop an Internet scavenger hunt by typing a list of simple questions that can be answered by exploring that site.
2. Find a class at another grade level to be buddies with your class.
3. Reproduce the scavenger hunt. Make enough copies for all of the students in your class and the buddies in the other class.
4. Discuss the activity with both classes at the same time. Talk about good strategies for working together on a project.
5. Pair each student in your class with a buddy from the other class.
6. Assign each pair of students to a computer.
7. Bookmark your chosen site on all of the computers so students do not have to look for it.

At the Computer

1. Open the Internet connection.
2. Go to the bookmarked site named on the Internet Scavenger Hunt.
3. Work with your buddy to find the answers to the questions.
4. Complete the Scavenger Hunt worksheet using answers that you find at the Web site.
5. Exit your Internet connection.

Extended Activities

1. This activity can be repeated using a different Web site and scavenger hunt each month.
2. You may wish to write the site that you used in your weekly or monthly parent newsletter so that students can further explore it if they have Internet access at home.

Wild Things

Software

- Any drawing software that allows you to add text

Skills Developed

- Drawing
- Fine motor
- Creative writing

Materials

- *Where the Wild Things Are* by Maurice Sendak (Harper & Row, 1963)

Template

- No template is needed.

Before the Computer

1. Read aloud *Where the Wild Things Are* by Maurice Sendak.
2. Talk about the fact that the wild things shown in the book are make-believe and the illustrator could have drawn them any way he imagined.

My wild thing has spots and sharp claws.

At the Computer

1. Open the drawing software.
2. Use the drawing tools to create your own, original wild thing. Remember to add details such as claws, sharp teeth, polka dots, and fur.
3. Type one or more sentences to describe your wild thing. Example: My wild thing has one eye and razor-sharp claws.
4. Print.

After the Computer

1. You may wish to make a display of the original monster creations.
2. As an alternative, put the monsters together into a class book. Place a copy of *Where The Wild Things Are* by Maurice Sendak in the resealable plastic bag with the class book. Encourage students to take the book home to share with their families.

Window Scenes

Software

- *Kid Pix* or *Kid Pix Studio*
- Any word processor

Skills Developed

- Drawing
- Fine motor
- Word processing
- Creative writing

Materials

- No additional materials are needed.

Template

- No template is needed.

Before the Computer

- No introductory activities are needed.

At the Computer

1. Open *Kid Pix* or *Kid Pix Studio*.
2. Choose the Wacky Paintbrush tool and select the open window option.
3. Click and drag the mouse to make a window that covers the entire screen.
4. Use the drawing tools and stamps to create a scene outside the window.
5. Print.
6. Open the word-processing software.
7. Type a story telling about the imaginary events that are taking place outside your window.
8. Print.

After the Computer

1. Display the window scene creations in your classroom windows. If you don't have any classroom windows, decorate a wall to look like windows. Then display the window scenes.
2. As an alternative, put the window scenes and window stories together into a class book. Have students take the book home to share with their families.

Wonderful Webbing

Software

- Any drawing software that includes stamps

Skills Developed

- Use of an idea web
- Word processing

Materials

- No additional materials are needed.

Template

- No template is needed.

Before the Computer

- Have each student choose a different stamp or graphic showing something about which they can brainstorm facts and information.

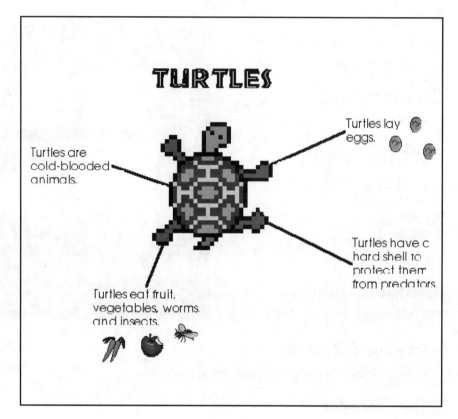

At the Computer

1. Open the drawing software.
2. Stamp your picture or place your graphic in the center of the screen.
3. Use a large type size to type the name of your picture at the top of the screen.
4. Type different facts and information about your picture around the screen.
5. Use your pencil tool to draw a line from each fact that you have typed to the picture in the center.
6. Choose stamps or graphics that relate to your facts and add them to your web.
7. Print.

After the Computer

1. Make a book of Wonderful Webs.
2. Students take this book home to share with their families.

Word-Processing Practice

Software
- Any word processor

Skills Developed
- Word processing
- Writing formal letters

Materials
- Chart paper or chalkboard
- Markers or chalk

Template
- No template is needed.

Dear Mom and Dad,

    Please come to our Open House on Thursday night. We have a lot of great things to show you. Our class has worked very hard this year. We would love to see you there.

Sincerely,
Sara

Before the Computer
1. Write important information such as time, date, and place for an upcoming event such as an open house.
2. Discuss how a formal letter begins with a greeting (Example: Dear _____ ,) and ends with a closing (Example: Sincerely, _____).

At the Computer
1. Open the word-processing software.
2. Type a formal letter to your parents inviting them to an upcoming school event. Remember to begin your letter with a greeting (Example: Dear _____ ,) and end with a closing (Example: Sincerely, _____).
3. Highlight all the text and choose a font size and style that is easy to read and that you like.
4. Print.

Extended Activity
- Your students can practice their word-processing skills by typing letters to inform their parents about field trips, school plays, and other special events. This is good practice for your students, and it may motivate them to be more responsible about showing notes to their parents.

Wrapping Paper

Software
- *Kid Pix, Kid Pix Studio,* or any drawing software

Skills Developed
- Fine motor
- Drawing

Materials
- No additional materials are needed.

Template
- No template is needed.

Before the Computer
- No introductory activities are needed.

At the Computer

1. Open *Kid Pix* or *Kid Pix Studio.*
2. Select a paint color and the Paint Bucket tool. Spill a solid or patterned background onto the screen.
3. Choose the Electric Mixer tool and experiment with all of the options at the bottom of the screen.
4. Print when your wrapping paper is complete.

   Note: Be sure to print more than one copy of your paper if you are planning to wrap a large gift.

Extended Activities
- If you do not have *Kid Pix* or *Kid Pix Studio* make wrapping paper using any drawing software. Decorate the page by drawing pictures or using stamps if they are available.

X-cellent Equations

Software

- Any greeting card software that allows you to custom-make cards

Skills Developed

- Beginning addition and subtraction
- Familiarity with greeting card software

Materials

- No additional materials are needed.

Template

- No template is needed.

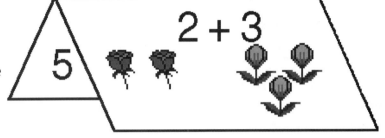

Before the Computer

- Provide a time for students to practice working with the greeting card software prior to this project.

At the Computer

1. Open the greeting card software.
2. Choose the orientation of the card if your software asks for this.
3. Go to the cover.
4. Type an addition or subtraction equation.
5. Stamp or draw a picture to illustrate your equation.
6. Go to the inside of the card and type or write the answer to the equation.
7. Print.

After the Computer

- Fold the printout like a card.

Extended Activity

- Display these "X-cellent Equations" in your classroom at a height that children can reach so that they can peek inside the cards for the answers to the equations.

Yellow Color Book

Software
- Any drawing software that includes stamps

Skills Developed
- Color recognition
- Color word recognition

Materials
- No additional materials are needed.

Templates
- Red Template
- Yellow Template
- Blue Template
- Green Template
- Purple Template
- Orange Template

Before the Computer
- No introductory activities are needed.

At the Computer
1. Open the word-processing software.
2. Find one of the color templates on the CD-ROM and import it into the drawing software.
3. Choose the Rubber Stamps tool.
4. Fill the screen with stamps that are the color of the color template.
5. Print.

After the Computer
1. Make a class book using students' pictures. Invite students to take home the books to share with their families.
2. As an alternative, students can make a page for each color and put the pages together to make their own books.

Yummy/Yucky

Software

- Any drawing software that includes stamps

Skills Developed

- Sorting
- Fine motor
- Stamp exploration

Materials

- No additional materials are needed.

Template

- Yummy/Yucky Template

Before the Computer

1. Explain what "yummy" and "yucky" mean.
2. Point out how some students might think a certain type of food is "yummy" while other students think the same food is "yucky."

At the Computer

1. Open the drawing software.
2. Find the Yummy/Yucky Template on your CD-ROM and import it into the drawing software.
3. Stamp or draw pictures of things that you think are yummy under the heading Yummy.
4. Stamp or draw pictures of things that you think are yucky under the heading Yucky.
5. Print.

After the Computer

1. Make a class book of yummy and yucky foods.
2. Have students take the book home to share with their families.

Zany Zoo

Software
- Any drawing software that allows you to add text

Skills Developed
- Drawing
- Fine motor
- Creative writing

Materials
- No additional materials are needed.

Template
- Zany Zoo Template

Before the Computer
- Explain what "zany" means.

At the Computer
1. Open the drawing software.
2. Find the Zany Zoo Template on the CD-ROM and import it into the drawing software.
3. Draw or stamp a zany creature that might be found in a zany zoo.
4. Type a few sentences describing your zany creature. Tell what it is called, what it eats, what kind of a home it lives in, and whether it gives birth to live young or hatches eggs.
5. Print.

The Zany Zoo

There's a purple space creature in my zany zoo.

Extended Activities
- You can display these pictures on a bulletin board entitled "The _____s' Zany Zoo." Fill in the blank with the correct grade level. Example: The First Graders' Zany Zoo.

Suggested Resources

Computer Books

Bennett, Steve and Ruth. *The Official Kid Pix Activity Book.* Random House, 1993.

Chan, Barbara J. *Kid Pix Around the World—A Multicultural Activity Book.* Addison Wesley, 1993.

Cowan, Bill. *Computer Basics.* Teacher Created Materials, Inc., 1995.

Gardner, Paul. *Internet for Teachers and Parents.* Teacher Created Materials, Inc., 1996.

Haag, Tim. *Internet for Kids.* Teacher Created Materials, Inc., 1996.

Hayes, Deborah. *Managing Technology in the Classroom.* Teacher Created Materials, Inc., 1995.

Lifter, Marsha. *Kid Pix for Terrified Teachers.* Teacher Created Materials, Inc., 1997.

Lifter, Marsha. *Writing and Desktop Publishing on the Computer (Primary).*
  Teacher Created Materials, Inc., 1996.

Children's Literature

Adams, Pam. *There Was an Old Lady Who Swallowed a Fly.* Playspaces, 1973.

Brown, Jeff. *Flat Stanley.* HarperCollins, 1989.

Carle, Eric. *The Very Hungry Caterpillar.* Philomel, 1969.

Christelow, Eileen. *Five Little Monkeys Jumping on the Bed.* Houghton Mifflin, 1989.

Heller, Ruth. *A Cache of Jewels and Other Collective Nouns.* Grosset, 1987.

Howe, James. *There's a Monster Under My Bed.* Atheneum, 1986.

LeSeig, Theo. *Ten Apples Up On Top!* Random, 1961.

Mayer, Mercer. *There's a Nightmare in My Closet.* Dial, 1968.

Mayer, Mercer. *There's an Alligator Under My Bed.* Dial, 1987.

McCracken, Marlene J. and Robert A. *Five Green and Speckled Frogs.* Peguis Publishers.

McKee, David. *Elmer.* William Morrow, 1989.

McMillan, Bruce. *Eating Fractions.* Scholastic, 1992.

Schmidt, Karen. *The Gingerbread Man.* Scholastic, 1967.

Sendak, Maurice. *Where the Wild Things Are.* Harper & Row, 1963.

Magazines

The Computing Teacher
ISTE
1787 Agate Street
Eugene, OR 97043

The Mailbox Magazine
1607 Battleground Avenue
P.O. Box 9753
Greensboro, NC 27429-0753

Technology and Learning
P.O. Box 49727
Dayton, OH 45449

Mail-Order Companies

Edutainment Catalog
(800) 338-3844, (303)444-3700 ext. 127
http://www.edutainco.com
Educational software at educational prices; volume discounts available.

Educational Resources
(800) 888-8399, (800) 624-2926
http://www.edresources.com
Educational software and hardware at educational prices; volume discounts and on-site training available.

Learning Services
(800) 877-9378, (541) 744-0883
http://www.learnserv.com
Educational software and hardware at educational prices; volume discounts available.

Learning Zone
(800) 381-9663, (206) 603-2570
http://www.zones.com
Educational software and hardware at educational prices; volume discounts and free phone technical support available.

MacWarehouse
(800) 255-6227, (800) 696-1727
http://www.warehouse.com
Educational software and hardware at educational prices; free phone technical support available.

Quality Computers
(800) 777-3642
http://www.sqc.com
Educational software and hardware at educational prices; volume discounts and free phone technical support available.